Two Italian Geniuses in New York
Broken American Dreams

CARMELO FUCARINO

Edited by Anthony Julian Tamburri
Preface by Joseph Sciame
Translation by Siân Gibby

CASA LAGO PRESS
NEW FAIRFIELD, CT

Diaspora
Volume 1

As **diaspora** *is the dispersion or spread of people from their original homeland, this book series takes its name in the intellectual spirit of willful dispersion of subject matter and thought. It is dedicated to publishing those studies that in various and sundry ways either speak to or offer new methods of analysis of the Italian diaspora.*

The publication of this book is due in part to a generous grant from the Sons of Italy Foundation, Washington, DC.

COVER ART: Garibaldi Meucci Portrait
by William J. Castello

Second printing, 2025

ISBN 978-1-955995-05-4
Library of Congress Control Number: Available upon request

© 2023 Text, Carmelo Fucarino
© 2023 Translation, Siân Gibby
© 2023 Preface, Joseph Sciame

All rights reserved.
Printed in the United States of America

CASA LAGO PRESS
New Fairfield, CT

Table of Contents

Preface, by Joseph Sciame (v)

Chapter 1 • There Was a Delta between Islands (1)

Chapter 2 • The Refugee Inventor (23)

Chapter 3 • The Adventure in Cuba (35)

Chapter 4 • The Gamble of New York (61)

Chapter 5 • The Invention of the Century (76)

Chapter 6 • The Hero of the Two Worlds: Precursor of the United Europe (108)

Chapter 7 • Cohabitation (124)

Postmortem • (153)

Bibliography • (171)

Index • (177)

About the Authors and Artist • (183)

Editor's Note

We are delighted to include this volume among the initial titles of Casa Lago Press. Carmelo Fucarino has been most gracious in offering us the opportunity to publish the English version of his book on Garibaldi and Meucci, a history of these two heroes who have not always gotten their just deserts. With this publication we can finally take stock of their parallel lives.

None of this would have been possible without our mutual friend Comm. Joseph Sciame and his introduction to Carmelo several years ago when Carmelo and his wife visited the United States. Since then, Carmelo and I realized that not only did we share mutual concerns about these topics and others, but that we have also published books with the same Italian press, Franco Cesati Editore of Florence, Italy.

Thank you finally to Sian Gibby for her keen editing skills in helping transform this book into a pleasant read and, as well, to Dr. Frances Curcio for his meticulous editing and reading for the historical facts of these two gentlemen in Staten Island.

Anthony Julian Tamburri
New York, April 15, 2025

Preface

Having met Professor Carmelo Fucarino some twenty years ago during his visit to the Garibaldi Meucci Museum and noting his sense of wonder and history, and each of us related in some way thru our roots in the *comune* of Prizzi, Province of Palermo, Sicily, I knew that one day he would capture the essence of two great men, Italians by birth and oftentimes considered Italian Americans by adoption. His words in this publication, *Two Italian Geniuses in New York: Broken American Dreams*, convey to the reader the "love" story of the deep relationships and friendships between General Giuseppe Garibaldi and Inventor Antonio Meucci, in which they each came with a dream of newness, success and a hope for happiness.

Faced with financial complexities of the times, each gentleman, clearly characterized by writer Fucarino, seeks the "American Dream," although broken at times by circumstances. A military hero recognized in Two Worlds, Garibaldi humbles himself to find work on his brief visit to Staten Island, New York, while Meucci continues with his plight for recognition of his "telefono."

Professor Fucarino documents the very precious pieces that even today are held at the historic Garibaldi Meucci Museum on Staten Island that provide the feeling of hospitality once rendered by the Meuccis, both Esterre and Antonio. What appears to be the main gift to readers of the lives of these two great men is an historic analysis of where they came from, what they did and accomplished, and how their memory through documentation is yet preserved today.

Professor Fucarino's prior comprehensive and extensive writings are topped by this most recent study, which evidences to the reader that despite the travails of the times, two men made history amidst their respective dreams. The book provides for us all a good lesson of today's changing world and challenges for each and every one!

Comm. Joseph Sciame,
President, *Sons of Italy Foundation*
Washington, D.C.

CHAPTER 1

THERE WAS A DELTA BETWEEN ISLANDS

April 17, 1524, was a splendid day. The carrack (the large sailing ship with bowsprit and three or four masts for square and lateen sails used by the Genoese for long ocean voyages), the one-hundred-ton flagship *Delfina*, or dolphin, named in honor of the eldest son of King Francis I of France, proceeded with a favorable wind into a pleasant inlet that was wooded on both sides. Little did the commander, Giovanni da Verrazzano, know that this was the wide mouth of a river, which ironically would later be named Hudson after the explorer Henry Hudson, the man who would reach it almost a century later in 1609.

Everything we know about this day we learn from a report sent on July 8, 1524, to Francis I,[1] who had granted Verrazzano

---

[1] Centro Studi Storici Verrazzano, via San Martino in Valle, Greti. Greve in Chianti (FI), online, "La lettera-relazione del luglio 1524" in which Giovanni da Verrazzano informs Francis I, King of France, of the successes of his exploration along the North American coast (from South Carolina to Nova Scotia). Dieppe, 8 July 1524.

four ships (in great secrecy), the other three called *Normanna*, *Santa Maria*, and *Vittoria*. The ships were in a race with Amerigo Vespucci (1454–1512) for Spain and with Ferdinand Magellan (1480–1521) for Portugal, searching for the free passage between the Atlantic and the Pacific. It was believed that the passage would lead to "those happy shores of Catai," this being the famous land that the Genoese Christopher Columbus (1451–1506) had left in search of with his three caravels. Two of Verrazzano's ships were lost in a storm, so the *Normanda* and the *Delfina* became "racing ships." Only the *Delfina* eluded Spanish and Portuguese surveillance and hid by a deserted islet (*Ilhas Desertas*) near the island of Madeira, on the night of January 17, 1524. She was sailing with a crew of fifty men, "provisions, weapons, and other war instruments and naval ammunition to last eight months." She moved, as Verrazzano wrote to the king, toward the west, borne by a "light and gentle wind that blew from the east," and traveled eight hundred leagues (about 4,800 km) in just twenty-five days. But on or around February 16, the ships ran into a violent storm the likes of which no one had ever seen before: "Only with divine help and thanks to the solidity of the ship with its glorious name and fortunate destiny (capable of resisting the powerful impact of the waves) were we able to save ourselves." Verrazzano continued his navigation west, with a slight deviation to the north, and in another twenty-five days he had covered more than four hundred leagues (about 2,400 km). Clearly, the crossing lasted more than the expected fifty days, as we read in the report of the coastal sighting:

> We came upon a land that had never been seen by ancient or modern man. When we got within a quarter league of it [about a mile and a half] we found that it was inhabited, judging by the very large fires burning on the beach. But we found no harbor or inlet to stop at and ended up dropping anchor offshore and sending a rowboat ashore. We spotted many people coming onto the

beach, but when they saw us approaching, they ran away. We tried to reassure them with gestures of various kinds, and some of them approached expressing great joy at seeing us, showing surprise at our clothes, our appearance, and the color of our complexion.

This took place on either March 7 or 8, and so it must have been Cape Fear, south of Wilmington.

This was Verrazzano's first encounter with the inhabitants of the new world: "They go completely naked, but they cover their genitals with the skins of small animals similar to martens attached to a belt of tightly woven grass with tails of other animals that, all around the body, hang down to their knees. The rest of the body and also the head they keep naked. Some, however, wear garlands of bird feathers. They are brown in color, not very different from the Ethiopians. They have thick black hair, not very long, which they wear behind their heads in the form of a pigtail. As for their figures, they are well-proportioned, of average stature, sometimes larger than ours, with a broad chest, strong arms, and well-structured legs and other parts of the body. They have large, black eyes and an attentive, lively gaze. They are not endowed with great physical strength but are of keen intelligence and are agile and very hardy runners. It was not possible for us to learn in more detail about their life and customs because we remained ashore for a short time and because there were only a few of who landed, leaving the ship anchored offshore."

From the coastline of fine sand, he could see the "beautiful countryside and plains covered with huge forests—in some areas sparse, in others thick—with trees of so many different colors, so beautiful and pleasant to look at, that it is difficult to put it into words. This land is rich in animals, lakes, and ponds of living water with various species of birds suitable to satisfy without difficulty all the sweet pleasures of hunting. The air is healthy, pure, and tempered by heat and cold. The sky is clear and serene, with rare rainfall."

Leaving the native settlement and seeing along the coast a large number of fires, he tried to land again with twenty-five men to obtain fresh water, but because of the gigantic waves it was impossible for him to reach the shore, where many people were rushing "showing to us signs of friendship and inviting us to land." Here, he reported to the king, a "stupendous episode" happened to him, which we repeat here: "We sent in one of our young sailors swimming to bring the natives some trinkets, such as rattles, mirrors, and small ornaments. When he came to a distance of four fathoms from land, he threw the objects on the beach and made to go back. But he was knocked over by a wave so violently that he fell unconscious and was washed ashore. Seeing this the natives rushed toward him and, taking him by the head, legs, and arms, carried him off a little way. Seeing himself transported in this manner, the young man, terrified, let out a great shout. And they did the same in their own language, signaling to him to calm down and be unafraid. Then they laid him down on the ground in the sunshine at the foot of a small hill and began to make great gestures of wonder. They looked with amazement at his white complexion, examined him well, took off his shirt and pants. After undressing him they lit a large fire and brought him closer to the flames.

Seeing this, the sailors who had remained on the boat became very frightened, as always happens to them when confronted by any novelty and thought that the natives wanted to roast him to eat him. The sailor, in the meantime, had recovered and after having remained for some time among the natives, he made them understand that he wanted to return to the ship. And they, expressing much affection and touching and embracing him, accompanied him as far as the shore and, in order to reassure themselves, climbed a high hill and followed him with their eyes until he got on the boat. They are black in color, very shiny skin, of average stature. They show little strength but an alert intelligence."

We may leave out his other sightings, as he headed first southward in search of a landing, reaching the northern end of Florida, and then going northward again "with anchors dropped offshore due to lack of ports in the area." Having continued along the coast, moving during the day, and dropping anchors at night, he spotted a land that he named *Arcadia* "for the beauty of the trees…. The area was very green and wooded, but without ports. From time to time, we could see beautiful headlands and small rivers.

"We saw a man approaching the beach to see what kind of people we were. He was guarded and suspicious. He was watching us, but not allowing us to approach him. He was handsome, naked, with hair gathered in a knot and olive colored. There were twenty of us on the ground, and by dint of flattery we managed to make him come up to about two fathoms from us, and he would show us a lighted piece of wood as if to give us the gift of fire. We, for our part, made a fire of dust with the tinderbox, and he trembled with fear. We threw a charge of the *schioppo* [musket]: he remained as if petrified and prayed, preaching like a monk. Pointing to the sky with his finger and looking at the ship and the sea, he seemed to want to bless us." It is difficult to establish which coast this was.

Verrazzano went on for another hundred leagues (600 km). He wrote, "We met a very beautiful place, situated between two hills in the middle of which flowed, toward the sea, a great river. We entered the river by boat and went ashore. We found it very populated. The natives were similar in appearance to the others. Dressed in bird feathers of various colors, they came to meet us cheerfully, emitting great cries of wonder and pointing out the best place to dock with the boat."

After another fifteen leagues (90 km) he reached another island where he found a "beautiful inlet," and where he saw "about twenty boats full of people who, shouting in wonder, surrounded the ship. They did not come within fifty paces, and, stopping, stared at the boat and at our appearance and clothes. Then all at once they gave a shout to show their contentment. We managed to reassure them a little by imitating their gestures, and then they came so close that we could throw rattles, mirrors, and various trinkets at them. They caught them, looked at them laughing, and, without any more fear came onboard the ship. Among them were two kings of such fine and vigorous appearance that it is difficult to describe them. The first was about forty years old; the other was a young man of twenty-four. They both dressed in the same manner. The elder on his naked body wore a deerskin worked like the fabrics of Damascus, with various embroideries. He wore nothing on his head, and his hair was gathered and tied behind his nape with various types of bindings. Around his neck he wore a wide chain adorned with stones of different colors. The clothing of the young man was similar." He passed on to describe the people as having the "fairest and mildest customs we found on the whole journey. In stature they are taller than we and are of the color of bronze, but some tend more to the white and others to yellow. The face is sharp, the hair is long and black, and they take great care of it, the eyes are black and darting, the appearance is sweet and suave in the manner of the ancients." He compares them almost to the beauty of classical sculptures. Also "their women are equally beautiful and well-formed, very gentle, elegant, and pleasant in appearance. Their costumes and feminine comportment are as good as can be asked of a human creature. They go naked wearing only an embroidered deerskin, like the men. Some of them wear precious lynx skins on their arms. They wear their heads uncovered with their hair in braids hanging down on either side of their chests. The adult married women wear hairstyles like those used by women in Egypt and Syria." His astonishment is so great that he even exalts their appearance and compares them to exotic images of women that perhaps he saw himself in his travels: "To their ears they wear pendants of all kinds, in the oriental manner, and this is the case of both men and women. Among other things, we noticed many worked copper sheets that they value more than gold. The latter is not valued because of its color. Of all metals, gold is the least valued because it is yellow, and they abhor yellow. The most loved colors are blue and red."

The gifts are always the same, those with which the conquistadors will exchange for gold jewelry: "Of the things we gave them they appreciated more the rattles, the blue crystals and other trinkets to put in their ears and neck. They showed no interest in draperies of silk and gold or any other kind, nor did they care to have them. The same thing happened with metals like steel and iron; several times we showed them our weapons, but they did not show interest in them, nor did they ask for them. They merely admired the ingenuity of their execution. They did the same thing with mirrors: they looked at them for a moment and laughing they returned them." He also got to experience their generosity and their being willing to give all that they have.

And so it was that "we formed a strong friendship with them. One day before we entered the inlet with the ship, we were forced by bad weather to drop anchor one league [6 km] off the coast. Then they came with a great number of boats up to the ship. Their faces were painted and smeared with various colors, and they looked cheerful and happy. They brought us their food and showed us where we were to throw the anchor, in the harbor, to secure the ship. They accompanied us in boats and stayed with us until we dropped anchor."

It was April 17, 1524, when Verrazzano entered the strait known today as "The Narrows" in the upper bay, which he christened "St. Margaret's," for the sister of Francis I. He landed at the tip of Manhattan and perhaps also at the farther coast of Long Island. His sojourn in the magnificent body of water was interrupted by a storm that pushed him north to Martha's Vineyard and then to find refuge in what today is called Newport.

During the fifteen days he remained in the inlet to replenish his supplies, from April 24 to May 6, "every day the natives came to see the ship, bringing their women with them. They are very jealous of them. When they came aboard the ship, even if they stayed a long time, they made the women wait in the boats. We begged them in every way, promising them all kinds of gifts, but they would not let them board the ship." He went several times five or six leagues [30 or 36 km] into the interior and found the land:

> of an indescribable beauty and suitable for all kinds of crops: wheat, wine, oil; because in them there are fields twenty-five to thirty leagues wide [150–180 km], open and without any impediment of trees and of such fertility that any seed would bear excellent fruit. As for the forests, they in one way or another can all be traversed even by a large army. In the forests grow oaks, cypresses, and other trees unknown in Europe. We found cherry trees, plum trees, hazelnut trees, and many types of fruit different from ours. There are many animals: deer, fallow deer, lynx, and other species that they, like the other natives, capture with bows and arrows, which are their main weapons. Their arrows are worked with great skill, putting in the point instead of iron emery, jasper, hard marble, and other sharp stones. They use these instead of iron to cut trees and build their boats from a single shaft of wood. With great skill they carve out of the trunk a concave surface in which fourteen to fifteen persons can comfortably sit. They have a short oar that widens at the tip that

they use at sea, relying only the strength of their arms, without any danger and giving the boat all the speed they want.

Penetrating the interior we saw their houses. They are built in a circular form of a size of fourteen or fifteen paces simply by superimposing trees bent in a semicircle and covering them with skillfully woven straw mats to shelter them from the cold and rain. There is no doubt that if they had such perfected tools as we have they would construct magnificent buildings. The entire coastline is full of cerulean, crystalline, and alabaster stones, which is why it is full of inlets and places of shelter for boats.

They move houses from one location to another depending on the fertility of the soil and on how long they have been in one place. They take away only the roofing mats and instantly have the new dwellings nice and ready. In each house live the father and his family, which can be very numerous. In some houses there are twenty-five to thirty people. They eat mostly legumes, like the other natives. But they produce them with more refined cultivation techniques, keeping in mind the lunar influence of the seeds, the location in the sky of the Pleiades, and many other elements indicated by the ancients. Also important to their diet are game and fish. They live long and rarely fall ill. If they are injured, they cure themselves with fire without complaining. We think they die mostly of old age. They have a strong sense of compassion and generosity toward their neighbors. In times of misfortune, they indulge themselves lavishly in lamentations, and in adversity they remember all the happy moments. When a relative dies they resort to a Sicilian-type weeping mixed with singing, prolonging it for a long time. This is what we could learn of them.

This was the astonished reception, in this moraine bay, of the Lenape natives (*lenni lenape* meaning "genuine man"), now of the Delaware Nation.

In the early days of July 1524, the expedition returned to Dieppe. The entire expanse of coastline from Florida to Cape Breton Island was named "Francesca." For his enterprise that gave luster to the Lily of France and lands to his king, but also for the precise and scientific location cartography of the inlet became known and disputed by enemy kings who asked for the work, but he remained faithful to Francis I. Born in the ancestral castle of Greve in Chianti on 1485, after two more crossings, Verrazzano died in the Abaco Islands in the Bahamas around 1528.

He had discovered and claimed for France that splendid inlet in which lay the islands that would later form the district of New York, but his name remained unknown. The entire continent came to be dedicated to Vespucci, while to Columbus the republic of Colombia (at the suggestion of Venezuelan patriot Francisco de Miranda), the union of American republics, and as well the capital of South Carolina (1799), Columbia, and Columbia University.

THE VERRAZZANO-NARROWS BRIDGE

Moreover, and despite his discoveries and the scientific cartography methods he inaugurated, Verrazzano received neither the honor nor the merit of the discovery of the inlet and the islands that today are the capital of the world. Only recently, in the 1950s and '60s, was he recognized as one of the greats of exploration, and, as a poor recompense, his name was given to the bridge over the inlet of New York, the Verrazzano-Narrows Bridge. It spans the Narrows, a body of water that links New York Harbor with Lower New York Bay and the Atlantic Ocean. As of December 1, 2020, the Verrazzano-Narrows Bridge became a two-way toll bridge, from Staten Island to Brooklyn and from Brooklyn to Staten Island. This came after a 34-year period in which tolls were collected only from Brooklyn to Staten Island.

The current bridge was opened to traffic for the upper level on November 21, 1964, and June 28, 1969, for the lower level. Each level has six lanes, a total of twelve for the bridge.

The idea for the project and the naming came in 1952 from the Italian American Historical Society with the support of James Angelo Kelly, a Brooklyn historian, and Jacques Herbert, historian and publisher of a French New York newspaper, and the efforts of John N. LaCorte, who prepared all the documentation for the recognition of the Italian explorer. The great success of the Society was the proclamation of April 17 as Verrazzano Day. However, the director of the Triborough Bridge and Tunnel Authority refused to accept the title in 1951: He had never heard of Verrazzano, and he thought the name was too long and difficult to spell and pronounce. But the effort finally was made possible by the unwavering will of Robert Moses (1888–1981).

Moses, a plenipotentiary and an unscrupulous urban planner of the "rip it up and start again" school, was responsible for the sweeping restructuring of New York between 1930 and 1970. His was a radical intervention that upset the structure of the Big Apple, with the demolition of dozens of largely low-income neighborhoods, sacrificed on the altar of progress. Whether Moses revived or ruined the city remains a Hamletian question, although Robert Caro's biography attempts to paint a complete picture.² The upheaval of nineteenth-century Paris was effected by Baron Georges Eugène Haussmann between 1852 and 1869, after which Palermo underwent the gutting of Via Roma between 1894 and 1936, and the various plans of Fascist Rome took shape. Moses began with parks, tree-lined streets connecting Long Island's prosperous suburbs, and swimming pools, some of which are still exemplars of modernist design. The Triborough Bridge, completed in 1936, radically reshaped the map of New York City. Holding power, though never elected, for the duration of twelve mayoral administrations, Moses promoted the two World's Fairs of 1939 and 1964. Between 1948 and 1952 he was responsible for development of the UN complex. His activity was controversial and opposed from a specific social point of view.³

It all seemed to be settled in 1960 when Governor Nelson Rockefeller signed the bill naming the bridge after Verrazzano. Yet, despite the categorical will of the "architect of New York," after John F. Kennedy's death thousands of signatures were collected of people asking to change the name of the bridge in his honor. John N. LaCorte telephoned US Attorney General Robert Kennedy, who vehemently assured him that the name would not be changed. LaCorte had met the attorney general with a request to recognize another Italian, Giuseppe Bonaparte, as the founder of the Federal Bureau of Investigation.⁴

The bridge was designed by eighty-year-old Swiss engineer Othmar Amman (1879–1965), who had designed New York

---

[2] The image of a Machiavellian man, racist in a series of anti-African American measures such as low bridge building, vindictive and without empathy is drawn from a 1975 biography by journalist Robert Caro, *The Power Broker: Robert Moses and the Fall of New York*, winner of the Pulitzer Prize and the Francis Parkman Prize and praised by the press as one of the best 100 books of the 20th century, "a modern Machiavelli prince" for *The Guardian*.
[3] See, Phillipe Martin Chatelain, Jane Jacobs, and Robert Caro.
[4] The new FBI Headquarters building Bonaparte Auditorium on Pennsylvania Ave in Washington, D.C., is named for him.

City's George Washington Bridge and the Golden Gate Bridge in San Francisco, and who was head of the New York Port Authority from 1930 to 1937. Until 1981 it was the longest-span suspension bridge in the world, 1,298 m, a record held until it was surpassed by the Humber Bridge in Kingston upon Hull (1,410 m) in the United Kingdom. The Verrazzano Narrows Bridge is supported by pylons of 27 thousand tons and towers that are 207 meters high, with a higher summit due to the curvature of the earth. Construction cost $320 million, and twelve thousand workers were employed on it. It served to connect the two military forts that protected the outer entrance to New York from the sea, Fort Hamilton on the Brooklyn side and Fort Wadsworth on the Staten Island side. It is open to pedestrians on the occasion of the marathon to Central Park, famous throughout the world for its 35,000 athletes who participate. Together with the Statue of Liberty it is an indispensable element of the city's skyline. Scenes from the film *Saturday Night Fever* starring John Travolta were filmed there.

A curious affair involved the spelling of the name *Verrazzano* as *Verrazano*, a spelling that was taken from sixteenth-century documents. After several attempts and appeals by Italian Americans such as Robert De Niro, on October 1, 2018, Governor Andrew Cuomo accepted the bill to change the name to *Verrazzano* with two z's. There are as many as ninety-six signs in the area with the old spelling that needed to be corrected, and you can imagine the astronomical cost of that undertaking: approximately $250,000. Hence the controversy and the priorities suggested for Staten Island's disastrous public transportation and the modernization of the metropolitan bus system. Therefore, the major entrance signs were corrected immediately while the others were to be replaced once they wore out.

Every year on April 17, Verrazzano Day is celebrated both

in New York and in his birthplace castle of Verrazzano in Greve in Chianti (Florence). Also dedicated to him is Maryland's Verrazzano Bridge, built in 1964 on Route 611 in Sinepuxent Bay to connect Assateague Island to the mainland. Yet another memorial is located in Rehoboth Beach in Delaware; it bears this inscription:

> In Commemoration of Verrazzano's Voyage to America
>
> Erected by the Delaware Commission on
> Italian Heritage and Culture
> 2008

STATEN ISLAND

Staten Island, about 155 square km in area, with 56 km of triangular-shaped waterfront, was not settled until 1683, when Richmond County was established there, one of the five administrative districts into which New York City was eventually divided, along with Manhattan, Brooklyn, the Bronx, and Queens.[5] It is one of New York State's original twelve counties. This occurred at the end of the Second Anglo-Dutch War in 1667 with the Treaty of Breda. The inhabitants remained loyal to the British, so much so that George Washington called them "our most inveterate enemies."

The first attempts at a permanent settlement of the island took place between 1639 and 1655 by the Dutch, who called the island Staaten Eylandt, from the name Staten Generaal, the parliament of the Republic of the Seven United Dutch Provinces. However, it was not until 1661 that a group of Huguenot Dutch refugees settled in the area called Oude Dorp (Old Town) to observe their religion. Here the first massacre of the natives was

---

[5] *Encyclopaedia Britannica*, s.v.

committed against all directives by Willem Kieft of New Netherland, the Dutch West India Company.

Until 1975 the Borough of Staten Island was officially called the Borough of Richmond, after Charles Lennox, the first Duke of Richmond and one of the first core of only 727 inhabitants. The borough was established as Staten Island in 1898 with the unification of New York City. To date, the "forgotten borough" is the least populated of the boroughs with 492,734 inhabitants, 55.7 percent white, of whom about 23.6 percent are Italian American and 19.6 percent Hispanic; other communities include Irish at 16 percent, Germans at nine percent, Poles, Russians, Albanians, and Asians between nine percent and three percent. People of color account for 11.6 percent, Native Americans a very small 0.7 percent. Median household income is approximately $98,000 to $76,000 with a poverty rate at 13.2 percent.[6]

Located southwest of Manhattan Island, Staten Island is separated from Long Island by the channel The Narrows, which Englishman William Howe crossed in August 1776 when he defeated George Washington at the Battle of Long Island.

Staten Island is the greenest in the area because of its organic system of public parks, the Staten Island Greenbelt. Yet until 2001 it was also used as New York City's largest public garbage dump; the 890-acre Fresh Kills Landfill is located on this estuary. Those who visited it in full operation remember with horror the stench and the danger of rampaging dogs. The landfill was opened at the end of the Second World War in 1948 with a temporary function, but as early as 1955 it had become indispensable, a hellish area unlike any other seen anywhere else in the world, not even in the suburbs of cities forgotten by civilization. It was used as the dumping place for 29,000 tons of

---

[6] *United States Census Bureau* (2021-2023) and the NYU Furman Center (https://furmancenter.org/neighborhoods/view/staten-island#demographics).

unsorted waste a day, with heaps reaching an average height of 30 to 70 meters. The waste disposal site was closed only at the end of 2001, after 53 years of activity, the result being the complete devastation of the area.

Plans are underway for a major cleanup and rebirth of the site. The Freshkills Park project began construction in October 2008, with the first section opening in 2012. When completed in 2036 it will be the largest developed park in New York City and nearly three times the size of Central Park.[7]

Yet it seems that New Yorkers can't forget the former function of their garbage dump, and still in recent years the nearly two million tons of concrete and steel debris extracted from the rubble of the World Trade Center's great pit at Ground Zero have been delivered there. Here amid the mass of material loaded from the Twin Towers were recovered fragments of bones and personal objects that were testament to the tragic memory of so many lives cut short. The area has the indirect privilege of being the largest public park dedicated to the memory of the only catastrophe of public buildings and human lives in the city's history, and of the United States in the modern age, as well as the physical remnant of war: an American version of the European cities destroyed in bombing raids in the previous century's wars. It opened again to allow for the placement of debris from the World Trade Center and Twin Towers disaster of that immemorial and historic September day and a resting place for the twenty-thousand fragments recovered of the 2,823 killed.

In addition to these particular and contingent functions, the urban history of the Borough of Staten Island from an architectural and housing point of view has undergone enormous changes starting from the seventeenth century. A fundamental

---

[7] More detailed information is available at the Freshkills Park website (https://www.nycgovparks.org/park-features/freshkills-park).

and unavoidable starting place is the ancient settlement, the historical center that today offers us in some parts a preserved example of the early colonial style. When I arrived there for the first time, not knowing what to expect, the cab took me to an avenue on which a series of single-family houses with flower beds in front presented themselves, surprising little houses in simple colonial style. Built in wood they dated back to the early twentieth century with their specific two-story (sometimes, but rarely, three) rectangular cusp façades. The style has been called Tudor or Victorian with Art Deco influences and can be seen in the residential area of Fort Hill, a knoll dotted with single-family cottages built between the nine-teenth and twentieth centuries. Also, in the area stands the St. George Theatre, a historic symbol of the island, and the City Council Building. In addition to Wagner College (founded in 1883 and relocated in 1918), there is a City University College and a major campus of St. John's University. The most important road is the Staten Island Expressway, the road that crosses the entire island and converges at the key point of the superb archway of the Verrazzano Bridge.

The main village consists of a large populous area that arose after World War II with the arrival of Hispanic Americans and people of color. The strong urbanization raises fears of a degradation of the urbanistic typicality, even in the neighborhood around Rosebank, where a low-key community settled casually in a largely Italian area that for generations seemed to remain contained. Chaotic development with add-ons on small spaces is changing the historic image, altering and defacing it with the congestion of houses unrelated to the storied context and the configuration of the avenues.

House Museum of Alice Austen
(1866–1952, one of the first women photographers,
eight thousand photos)

A BRIGHT SUNNY DAY

Yes, it was a beautiful, bright spring day when I crossed the Verrazzano-Narrows Bridge in amazement and delight. And then the tour of the island searching for the cottage of an Italian American professor who had invited me at first sight in a fleeting encounter during the closing evening of the academic year at St. John's University. It was an evening, of course, of music, including tenors and sopranos and music of Italian folklore.

The taxi driver was determined to find the address himself. We searched for hours until realizing that the easiest solution was to contact the professor, Joyce, by phone. She welcomed me with her poodle, Baci.

Yet, it had been useful to make contact with that coastline all around the island. It was contact with the typical cottages, the porches, the wooden structures in addition to that first meeting in the Chinese Scholar's Garden. That would come later, when I was accompanied by St. John's University administrator Joseph Sciame for a visit to the Museum.

Italy seemed great to me, and the Museum stirred my Sicilian memory of *picciotti* and red shirts, and of the "duce" that I knew in his poncho.

IN ROSENBANK THE COTTAGE

The Rosenbank neighborhood was originally called Peterstown, then Clifton. It took on the appellation of Village of Edgewater for the first time after 1880. Wealthy landowners claimed large estates there along the coast and inland of the island. Most of the wooden cottages are three-story, flat-roofed Italianate style and are arranged in rows along the sidewalk, detached from their neighbors, but not so detached as to compromise that close relationship. Building speculation, accentuated by immigration of Filipinos and Hispanics, led in the 1960s to the demolition of many old houses and the construction of new row houses of beige brick and stucco. In the 1980s, a fourteen-story skyscraper with a heated outdoor swimming pool sprang up at 31 Hylan Boulevard.

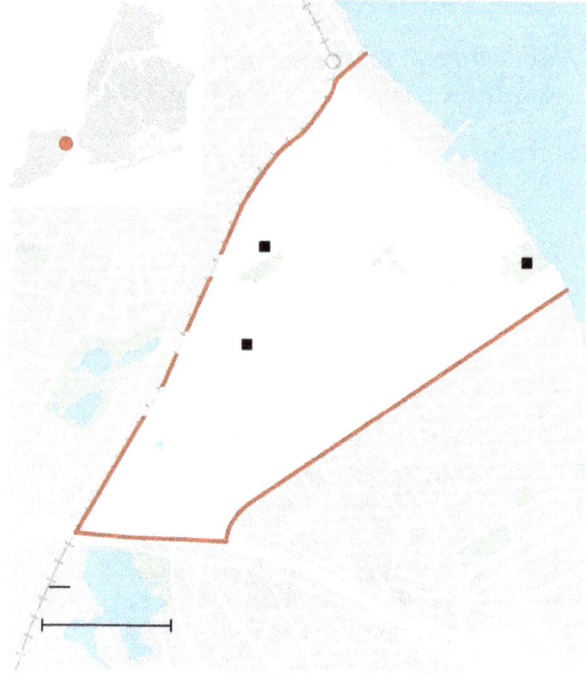

The Archdiocese of New York maintained the St. Mary's School until deciding, in 2011 and with an enrollment of 224 students, to close it, despite it being one of the oldest Catholic school facilities on Staten Island. The closing is believed to have been a consequence of infrastructure problems. In 2013 St. Joseph's School also closed. St. John's Episcopal Church, dating back to 1843, embodies a Catholic-influenced devotion that is also visible at the Our Lady of Mount Carmel Grotto. This local shrine was a community effort, built in 1937 and subsequently enlarged by volunteers from the Society of Our Lady of Mount Carmel, a mutual aid society established on February 28, 1903. This community spirit is further demonstrated by the nearly annual celebration held since 1903. The eight-day event starts on July 13 and takes place on Amity Street, with the main celebration occurring on July 16. Musical entertainment at the grotto, which is on the National Register of Historic Places, will include an Elvis impersonator (Sciorra).[8]

---

[8] Dr. Joseph Sciorra is director of Academic and Cultural Programs at Queens College's John D. Calandra Italian American Institute, ethnologist, and author of *Built with Faith: Italian American Imagination and Catholic Material Culture in New York City*, and co-editor of the two-volume anthology *New Italian Migrations to the United States*.

As at Ellis Island, this neighborhood had been a federal quarantine station for incoming immigrants, a facility that only closed in 1971. Also, during World War II, one of the many internment camps for Italian prisoners was built in a marginal wetland area (Staten Island 350th Anniversary Committee); today it houses the seventeen-acre Eibs Pond Park (Rosebank Hughes).

With the growth of immigration came allotments of small estates where Italian immigrants came to settle; their descendants became over time a predominant ethnic group, forming a real Little Italy on the island.

This explains how in the heart of the neighborhood, right where Italian immigration was most intense, at 420 Tompkins Avenue, a Gothic-style cottage built in 1840 was moved here from its original location nearby in 1907 and eventually transformed into a Garibaldi Memorial.

Chapter 2

The Refugee Inventor

The Rebel of the Grand Duchy of Florence

Carlo Lucarelli, a screenwriter and journalist best known to television audiences for his detective investigation program, *Blu note misteri* d'Italia, gives us a picture of the scientist Antonio Sante Giuseppe Meucci as put forth by Lucarelli's own grandmother, who "proudly called herself a 'Meucci'":

> In my house this indicated two very specific things. On the one hand, it expressed the pride of those who knew they were descended from a great inventor, from the "man who invented the telephone," as she said. On the other, the awareness of belonging to a lineage of "romantic losers," that of the Meucci family. Intelligent, intuitive, rebellious, but completely lacking in the so-called "bump" for business. They were people of genius, not of industry.... His inventions were not born from the desire to make a business out of them, but from the pleasure of "playing" with modernity. He had an instinct that I would define as "futuristic," which attracted him to new technologies. The result? He found himself without the $250 needed to file the patent that Alexander Graham Bell (1847–1922), a Scottish scientist and inventor who emigrated to the USA and who for decades took credit for the invention, instead did have. My grandmother concluded. "The Meuccis are all dummies. They don't have their feet on the ground." (Rotondi)[9]

Meucci was born at 5:00 in the afternoon of Wednesday, April 13, 1808, in the village of San Frediano in Florence, the son of thirty-two-year-old Amadigi and twenty-two-year-old Maria

---

[9] Carlo Lucarelli dedicated to Meucci an episode of DEE Giallo on February 21, 2011. First film *Antonio Meucci. Il mago di Clifton-del1940*, dir. Enrico Guazzoni, starring Luigi Pavese.

Domenica Pepi.[10] The eldest of nine children, he was baptized in the Baptistery of S. Giovanni. In memory of the scientist's birth, the city placed a commemorative plaque at the site in 1996.[11]

Via de' Serragli, 44

In November 1821, at the age of thirteen, he was admitted to the Academy of Fine Arts in the section Elements of Figure Drawing, which he attended for six years. This was a school of European excellence, whose field of study, in addition to the curricular subjects of art and literature essential in all technical courses, also covered other disciplines unrelated to design, such as engineering, chemistry, and mechanical physics with emphasis on the areas of acoustics and electricity. These new

---

[10] Baptismal registration in the Archives of the Opera di Santa Maria del Fiore, Florence.
[11] See, Basilio Catania (1994); "Antonio Meucci" in *radiomarconi.com*; and *Dizionario Biografico degli Italiani* s.v.

disciplines had been introduced during the Napoleonic era (1799-1815). These disciplines played a part in the future choices and insights of Meucci and went beyond the specific fields of drawing and art.

Meucci's father, Amadigi, a supernumerary customs officer in the garrisons at the gates of Florence, obtained for his fourteen-year-old boy on May 12, 1824, an assignment as an assistant customs officer at the "Custodia delle porte" at Porta di S. Niccolò for passport control.

His path, however, began to become more clearly marked out the following year on the occasion of the party for the imminent birth of Grand Duchess Maria Carolina of Saxony, when the boy was co-opted by the impresario Girolamo Trentini as an assistant to the preparation and launching of fireworks. Everything went smoothly in the first two evenings, but on the third, April 4, 1825, due to the powerful mixture of propellant he had employed, the rockets escaped his control and ended up on the houses in front of the Palazzo Vecchio, causing damage as well as injury to the spectators. The law-enforcement tribunal that dealt with the investigation of a serious suspicion of conspiracy, exonerated him along with his two colleagues by giving them the benefit of the doubt.

This tribunal had been instituted in Florence on May 15, 1680, by an order of Grand Duke Cosimo III dei Medici: "Appresso a questo tribunale della Ruota risegga ogni autorità, balia, e giurisdizione delle cause criminali privativamente o cumulativamente con altri Tribunali e Magistrati come sta e resiede di presente nel Magistrato degli Otto, circa i delitti di qualunque sorte e qualità che si commetteranno nella città e nello stato (eccettuati gli casi e cause come sopra riservate e destinate al magistrato degli Otto, eccettuate le cause di Pistoia e sua montagna, Pontremoli e Siena" (Cantini, 148).

Another incident in June did not result in the same way

when Meucci's negligence in not having nailed a door shut in front of a ditch, where his colleague Luigi Ficini subsequently fell and fractured his leg, was recognized. This time he was imprisoned. He was sentenced to eight days, the first three of which on bread and water.

The convict was invited to present himself at the police station, at five o'clock in the evening, on pain of being fined fifty lire (about fifty dollars), which was a heavy fee for a worker of the times. So Amatis went with a seventeen-year-old Antonio to the commissary Calleni on the evening of June 4. Antonio was stunned and overcome with shame at the thought of what the great professors Gori and Calamandrei and his wealthy companions at the academy would have said and thought. It is said that Calleni, putting his arms on the father's shoulders, almost weeping, heartened him by saying: "Che thu thi preoccupi, Amàto, che il thu figliolo mangia a spese del Granduca per qualche jiòrno?" To which he replied: "What about the three days of bread and water? And the mark of prejudihato." And the friend who had seen the boy grow up and now found him equal to his father advised him, since he was a master of how to write to those on high, to write a plea "tearful and obsequious" and "full of good intentions" and he would see that they would reduce his sentence. The plea to the Magistrate of Good Government, who then had the direction of the Florence police, resulted in his serving only five days.

This was not the last occasion of imprisonment in his tenure as customs officer, which lasted from 1823 to 1830. Transferred in 1826 from his home in Porta S. Gallo, he went to prison again in 1829 for a personal matter having to do with women: Enamored of the daughter of the tractor and corresponding with her, he aroused the wrath of a certain Nibbio, whom he then provoked with insults, and in the end, he left the service. He was therefore accused of abandonment of work. When he revealed the reasons for having left, he was constrained to return to prison from May 2 to June 1, 1829, and also suffered the suspension of salary, the payment of expenses, and the prohibition to approach the woman in question. He later went back again to prison for refusing to adhere to the last of these rules. Again, he was given the charge of delaying work. By this point he was now being watched. It is true that in those days in Florence they did not go easy on the use of prison. Clearly Meucci was also looking for trouble.

Eventually he lost his patience and on July 13, 1830, resigned, but it wasn't long before he petitioned the Magistrate of Good Government to be rehired as assistant customs officer.

As if these trivial accidents, carelessness, or just bad luck were not enough, he joined the Carbonari in those years. He was twenty-two years old when, in February 1831, the Carbonari uprisings broke out in Emilia-Romagna, led by Ciro Menotti. Meucci already showed his sympathy for Mazzini's thought and joined the Giovine Italia. For this cause, he ended up in prison for three months, along with Mazzini and Francesco Domenico Guerrazzi (1804–1873), who in February 1849 fled the Grand Duke. Guerrazzi was famous also for his novels and especially for *Beatrice Cenci*.

Meucci's descendent Lucarelli writes: "He was 23 years old when, enraged by the insurrectionary movements of '31 that were shaking Italy, he tore up the photos of the Grand Duke of Tuscany Leopold II under the eyes of the police" (Rotondi, 16-21).

In 1833, having lost his job at the customs office, and in search of an occupation that was not oppressive and that could become a source of new ideas, Meucci saw a way out in trying work in the theater. He quickly understood that this was an activity that could fulfill his artistic, as well as creative, leanings compared to the tedious and risky career of a customs officer. In this occupation he would also have had time and the opportunity to carry out other activities and to work in the evening, as well as certainly more freedom and inventiveness. He had already worked as a boy occasionally as an assistant props maker for a few evenings at the Teatro Giglio (formerly the Teatro della Quarconia[12]), which was also open in summer, although of poor reputation. Other evenings he had spent at the Theater Alfieri, founded in 1740 from the Academy of the Risoluti, and the Theater Goldoni, founded by the impresario Luigi Gargani and inaugurated in 1817. He had also done some occasional evening work at the more prestigious Teatro della Pergola.

The perfect opportunity to put his professionalism to good use and fulfill his aspirations was offered to him in 1833 by the custodian of the Teatro della Pergola, Dante Margheri, who had advised him to return toward the end of the year to contact the impresario of the theater, the legendary Alessandro Lanari, because he was currently traveling around Europe in search of talent to sign up for the new season which began in December. A native of Marche, Lanari had begun his career as impresario of the Teatro del Giglio in Lucca in 1821 at the age of thirty-one and was considered the greatest impresario of the time. He had been working at La Pergola for two years, where he would

---

[12] It later became the National Cinema and was originally the Hospice of the Quarconia or Casa dei Monellini, or the Hospice of San Filippo Neri. It was the first charitable reformatory in Florence, a shelter for "vagrant" orphans, founded in 1659 by Filippo Franci, an artisan eyeglass maker and friend of Grand Duke Ferdinando II de' Medici. The Tabernacle of the Quarquonia, where San Filippo Neri presented the young children to the Virgin, was a testimony to this. In 1787 Gioacchino Cambiagi founded the theater of Quarquonia, a place for popular entertainment, with recitals in the vernacular where he debuted the Florentine mask of Stenterello, the mask of Florence. In 1826 it was called Teatro del Giglio, in 1840 Teatro Leopoldo for a cultured and refined public. With the Kingdom of Italy became the National Theatre for brilliant comedies. In 1919 it was the seat of the first national congress of the Fasci where the young Mussolini praised the March on Rome. In the post-war period, it became the National Cinema again.

remain until his death in 1862. It was said of him that he was an extraordinary discoverer of talent but also a wise administrator and a refined diplomat with the powerful.

Margheri also informed him that Artemio Canovetti, the current chief machinist, was looking for someone who had attended the Academy, "because he was tired of the idlers who pretended to be expert toolmakers, without possessing the slightest notion of mechanics."

It was his snapshot of a theater that was in the top tier of world for theatrical technique and stage equipment. Therefore, in July 1834, he became Canovetti's assistant props maker and Lanari's trusted man.[13] He acquired excellent experience in the field, putting his technical studies to good use, dealing with almost everything concerning stage technique in props, from physics to electrical works, from mechanics and chemistry to optics, as well as stage art.

The Teatro della Pergola has enjoyed until the present a glorious history of great professionalism and prestige. It was built in wood in 1656 by the architect Ferdinando Tacca, commissioned by Cardinal Giovan Carlo de' Medici, president of the Accademia degli Immobili, and therefore it became "teatro granducale." It was inaugurated during the carnival of 1657 with an opera buffa. But it was completed only in 1661 in celebration of the wedding of the Grand Duke Cosimo III to Margherita Luisa d'Orléans.

The teatro was an architectural miracle, as the first large theater "Italian style," that is, with tiers of boxes on top of each other and not, as was typical, with decreasing semicircular tiers, with a series of raised seats, supported by columns. For a more perfect acoustic performance, the oval shape of the structure was experimented with for the first time. The teatro had a large

---

[13] Exchange of four letters now in the National Library of Florence. See, Catania (1994, 159).

stage with an elegant arch, three tiers of boxes supported by a loggia open on the stalls where the fixed benches formed two sectors separated by balustrades and intended to keep separate the male and female audience members. At the center of the room was the stage with the throne of the cardinal and his guests. The boxes, comfortable in their "intimacy," were noisy and places of excessive dinners.

The building underwent various renovations: in 1688 with the addition of a fourth tier of boxes; in 1718 it became the property of the Academy with the support of Grand Duke Cosimo III. The biggest change, however, took place between 1753 and 1755, when it was rebuilt entirely in masonry, saving it from the danger of fire which was always lurking, given the use at the time of a large quantity of candles to give splendor to the halls and the stalls.

In 1789, a fifth tier of boxes was added. Between 1800 and 1804 the music room, today's "Saloncino," was built in the building on the east side. The interventions of Bartolomeo Silvestri (1820 and 1828) and Gaetano Baccani in 1855–1857 with the construction of the entrance and the vestibule, gave it its present structure. At this stage it is said that Meucci installed there the first acoustic telephone in history, with mechanical not electric transmission to communicate with the different areas of the theater. Between 1837 and 1847 Alamanno Biagi was the director of the orchestra, although Lanari preferred Luigi Maria Viviani.

When the first stagehand, Canovetti, accompanied him to the impresario, Meucci was shocked by his appeal: "You will take up your duties this evening, in two hours, as a toolmaker and machinist in aid to the second machinist, Mr. Corsi, both employed by Mr. Canovetti. Your commission is 40 lire per week, but only for the season. I will find you another job for the summer. You can stay for free in a room of the machinists' apartments. Canovetti will show you. That's the closet for his tools. If you do well, you will be able to become second stagehand in a year's time. You will follow my crew on tours to various cities: we have contracts for Rome, Livorno, Ancona, Foligno, and Naples. Good luck!"

He was very shocked to have suddenly found a well-paid job and an accommodation that took him out of poverty. He was even more astonished by Canovetti addressing him formally, which he had never experienced at his age and in the humble work in customs: "Mr. Meucci, we don't need you tonight. Come tomorrow morning to my place ... How about ten o'clock? Bring your things, so you can settle in here... Go... Go... And ... congratulations!"

It was the most exalting achievement of his life. The theater is the most extraordinary invention that Greek civilization could implement, the word and action that come to life to achieve perfect mimesis, from that mythical chariot of Thespis to the powerful rituality of Aeschylus's theater and up to the perfection of Sophocles, who enlarged and defined the actors and the choral elements and above all introduced scenography, which was missing until him and remained rather allusive. In the new modern theatrical performances, this had a fundamental function such that together with vocality and gestures it also became visual language, that is, the sum of additional languages, such as painting, sculpture, decoration, which, in the interaction of different structures and images, become the expressive power of verbal communication. Therefore, in Western civilization, theater in its various forms has become the perfect form and poetic synthesis of the expression of life, relationship, and pathos.

In the words of Gaetano Oliva: "Scenography develops through the interaction of several structures and images; light, sounds and, sometimes, even movements act in it. It is defined, therefore, through a chorus of different interventions and possesses an autonomous expressive potential that is too often underestimated. One of the most important elements in the process of forming a set design is undoubtedly the image. Aware of its enormous importance in society, scenography enhances its communicative and relational value. It is a fundamental and immediate stimulus; through its intentional placement within a scenography, it also becomes a didactic and educational element. Scenography is, by definition, the complex of elements, artistic and technical, that contribute to creating the environment in which the scene takes place, whether it be theatrical or cinematographic" (Oliva, 18-19).[14]

This new working approach offered Meucci motivation and impulses for the insights that would be expressed in this supreme genius of creation. One of the many opportunities he

---

[14] Gaetano Oliva teaches History of the Theatre and the Performing Arts, Dramaturgy, Animation Theatre, Organization and Economics of the Performing Arts at the Faculty of Education of the Università Cattolica del Sacro Cuore in Piacenza, Milan and Brescia. He is the artistic director of the Center for Theatre Research "Theatre-Education" of the City of Fagnano Olona.

encountered in his work was the distances of the operations on the immense stage. Considering the difficulty in communicating and being heard from the stage floor to the maneuvering grid located about eighteen meters high, he invented the first acoustic tube, which he embedded in the wall for convenience. The invention was greeted with great amazement and satisfaction by the stagehands, who could work more easily and safely at a height of about twenty meters. In his time stagecraft, that is, the art of organizing and realizing the scenography, was quite arduous and tiring because it was all done by hand using ropes, nails, and glue in an environment illuminated by torches. Apart from the tools used to set up the structures according to the indications of the director and the set designer with the use of sketches, the task of the stagehand was fundamental. In every field of staging, professionalism was acquired through daily practice. Agility and physical vigor were necessary for the ceiling technician who worked on the grid and took care of the pitches. At the time, nails were collected and the ability of the technician to rework and modify the material used was important. Now everything is made simpler and easier with the use of computers and the adoption of sophisticated systems of counterweights, nails are bought new, and the scenes are made in detail in polystyrene and fiberglass as disposable material.

Imagine Meucci who, in the most up-to-date and renowned theater in the world, had a simple closet as a workroom for his tools and for his scenic creations.

And then came the magical evening of the premiere. Let's imagine the arrival of the carriages, the rustling of the silks, and the clouds of the ladies' perfumes in the immense and luxurious entrance of the Pergola, while behind the scenes there is the fervor of prop makers and designers, costume designers, laborers. And the magic of the show. Then the roar of applause, the encores, the fall of the curtain, while the audience swarms to the exit and the hall falls empty and silent and the operators of the scene finish their work. That evening, the costume designer Maria Matilde Ester Mochi, in the splendor of her beauty and her twenty-four years, lingers to put the costumes in order. Then she takes the initiative, approaches Antonio, and asks him if he can accompany her home: She is afraid to go home alone. She knows Antonio lives in the theater, he says he lives there, but he'd like to take a walk, he's not sleepy and he's too tense with the fear that something hasn't gone right. He was thunderstruck by the young woman's beauty and refinement, but he was far from thinking that such an exceptional girl and accomplished artist could notice a cheap prop maker who had just arrived and of whom she knew nothing. She told him about her situation, the death of her father, her work and everyday life. In front of S. Maria Novella, she said, "You see, Mr. Meucci, if anyone ever wants me as a bride, he will take me to the altar in this church."[15]

Here they would be married on August 7, 1834, with an ecclesiastical rite, this prop maker and costume designer. However, as in the hidden wedding of Renzo and Lucia in *I promessi sposi*, they did not publicize the event, to avoid complications with the law, and revealed mere traces of their address.

From that day on they would live together for better or worse and in both worlds for almost fifty years.

---

[15] His fictional biography, on the trail of the biography of Basil Catania.

CHAPTER 3

THE ADVENTURE IN CUBA

And then something happened, unimaginable and unexpected, the great turning point in the life of the bizarre and brilliant Florentine. And it was a lucky chance due to his passion for Italian opera, which was then and still today is the symbol and the myth of bel canto. During one of my cab rides to New York's Kennedy Airport, the cab driver, hearing my Italian speech, mentioned the aria *Nessun Dorma* and went crazy for our Sicilianness, to the point of calling his mother on the phone to announce in a tenor voice the presence of a fellow countryman, a fellow citizen of Verdi and Puccini. But at the time of Meucci's arrival, opera throughout America was more widespread and popular, because that was the "show," with that music par excellence recreating events of love and death. There was no other musical stardom. Jazz had yet to be invented.

TACÓN'S DREAM

This passion, which made itself felt in the fanaticism of wealthy Cubans for opera, inflamed the soul of the dynamic Don Miguel Tacón y Rosique (1775–1847) of Cartagena and spurred him to action.

Appointed by Ferdinand VII, on June 1, 1834, he had settled in Havana as captain general, that is, as governor, replacing Mariano Ricafort Palacin y Abarca (1776–1846). In 1847, for his abilities, he would be named Duke of the Union of Cuba in honor of Isabella II.

We must immediately say that equally revolutionary for those times and in a colony were his other initiatives concerning public works and the modernization of the country, such as the construction of the first railway and the urban aqueduct.

When he arrived, Cuba had just emerged from a serious cholera epidemic and at the end of a phase of civil unrest with the return of the liberals from exile. In order to re-establish order, however, Tacón had to intervene with iron discipline and with effectively authoritarian methods, and his management garnered high praise and recognition in 1837, but it also drew fierce criticism and antipathy.

In this strong desire to establish a climate of pacification and social stability, he believed that art, even merely the enjoyment of spectacle, could promote and encourage the balance desired. The first request that don Miguel Tacón made in the year of his arrival to the minister of the interior of the Spanish Crown was authorization to build a large opera house, an ambitious project that was intended to bring prestige to the island. He must have believed in the effectiveness of the idea, or at least been passionate about this art that was then the symbol of music and Italianism in the world.

Jacobo de la Pezuela thus explained the reasons why Tacón decided to build the new theater. The capital in 1834 had in fact only one Coliseo, the Teatro Principal, which, located at the far end of the city, was difficult to reach because of its distance, and it also had a small capacity. De la Pezuela says that he was "determined at the end of that year to promote the opera of a more central and adequate theater for dramatic and musical representations"; and such was the situation that for many years the taste of the region's opulent families for the musical spectacles was very pronounced, and no good company of Italian opera could be invited without the wealthy aficionados to support it. Up to this point it was only the rich ones who were able to enjoy their preferred entertainment. These reasons induced Tacon in 1835 to undertake the work of its vast and elegant theater in one of the choicest locations in the city. And Don Francisco Marty y Torrens had undertaken the contract and the construc-tion of the building and the nurseries of the Pescaderia (de la Pezuela, 177).

THE MAGICAL MARTI, THE FACTOTUM OF L'ABANA
In order to realize his passion, Don Miguel Tacón was lucky enough to meet the right man. He was the man for all occasions, one who would stop at nothing and who would become the most powerful man on the island and beyond.

He was the Catalan Don Francisco Marty y Torrens (Ramiez, 137–146), popularly known in Cuba as "Pancho Martí." He was also well known between Catalonia and Cuba as a very rich and enterprising businessman, with extraordinary intuition and intelligence in the field, including a flair, cunning, and lack of scruples in line with the customs of the time, which is to say that he was involved in the slave trade, and possibly also with brazen and reckless piracy. With this theater project, his business would have benefited by the acquisition in vast real estate and agricultural farms in which he employed his slaves. He became the governor's right-hand man. He was also the owner of two shipyards where ships involved in clandestine traffic were repaired. The governor also granted him, over the protests of the City Council, a lifetime monopoly on the fish trade in Havana, for the marketing of which he built the Pescadería del Boquete, which opened in 1836 behind the Cathedral of Havana and was active until 1895. On the same premises he lived, enjoying his immense wealth, until he settled on the Paseo del Prado between Animas and Trocadero, where he died on May 29, 1866.

About this project, musician and conductor Max Maretzek recounts that he doesn't know much, yet he has some insights (1855, 149–221). He observed that cities as large as Boston, Philadelphia, Cincinnati, and Baltimore, with populations equal to Vienna, Naples, Berlin, and Milan did not have a "regular Italian Opera." He indicated as an exception in North America (besides New York City) the island of Cuba and explained that this was on account of Don Francisco Marty: "It is said, then, that in his younger days, the Havanese impresario was the friend of a most formidable pirate[16] who plagued the Mexican Gulf and the seas immediately adjacent to it. The Spanish government offered a large reward for the capture of this pirate. Immediately, the youthful Francisco felt it his duty to serve his government. The pirate fell into a trap, which was very neatly laid for him, and was taken. He was subsequently 'garoted,' this punishment being a peculiarly agreeable and expeditious way of executing a prisoner in public, which is in vogue in Cuba. As his recompense, the amiable Francisco received the privilege of all the fish markets in the island. Nobody in all Cuba had the right of selling a single fish without paying certain dues to Don Francisco Marty y Torrens. In addition to this, he had money. How much or where acquired, no one knows. This cash he invested in building or chartering some hundreds of fishing boats. He was therefore enabled, after a short time, to supply his own markets" (Maretzek 1855, 151).

In this monopolistic regime, "This business, in which he could encounter no opposition, soon afterwards took on under his management such colossal proportions that, some years later, its annual profits were estimated at 10,000 ounces of gold, or something equivalent to 800,000 francs. Still retaining a certain predilection for everything approximating to his old profession (you note, I presume, the delicate name with which it is characterized), he fitted out several large vessels to carry

---

[16] It was in 1830, in command of his ballander *La Esperanza*, when he captured the schooner *Rosario* of the pirate Antonio Moriño, in the Cayo Cruz del Padre. He received from the king as a reward the rank of Ensign of Frigate.

on the slave trade. His baits were now firearms, doubloons, and kegs of brandy. His hooked fish were now negroes from the coast of Africa and Indians from Yucatan. These the bribed authorities of the island permitted to be landed and sold there. This speculation increased Marty's fortune, and it soon reached an almost fabulous extent. He now dabbled in government securities and was several times called on to help the government of Spain out of its momentary embarrassments. For this devotion a payment had to be received, and it was offered to him in the shape of knighthood and 'letters of nobility' by the Spanish crown. Thus, he became not only powerful in Havana, but great also in Madrid, in which city he keeps his regular agents" (Maretzek 1855, 152). The choice of Marty as assignee of the works and impresario of the theater proved how near to him were the economic and speculative interests in the construction of the new Coliseo, which complemented his other entrepreneurial activities.

The idea of founding the new theater, according to Maretzek, had arisen as a revenge against the hatred that the Castilian nobility nurtured against him for his shady dealings, so much so that he had succeeded in having the contract revoked by Captain General José Gutiérrez de la Concha, Marquis of Havana: "The proud Castilian nobles of the island absolutely refused to tolerate the slave-dealer and fish seller in their society. He therefore determined upon forcing them to swallow the fish and digest the negro. To do this, he built a splendid Opera House, engaged first-rate Opera troupes, and became his own Manager" (1855, 153).

Maretzek added that "in the summer of 1850, however, the greatest *troupe* which had ever been heard in America was sent to this city. Indeed, in point of the integral talent, number, and excellence of the artists composing it, it must be admitted that it has seldom been excelled in any part of the Old World....

The greater portion of them enjoy a wide and well-deserved European reputation, and their reunion, anywhere, would form an almost incomparable Operatic troupe" (1855, 156). It is not said whether it was the Compagnia di La Pergola of Florence, but it was reported that among the prima donnas and tenors in the group was the famous Salvi.

This is how Marty Jacobo de la Pezuela presented it in his *Diccionario*: "This intelligent speculator discovered a lucrative future in the planned theater and therefore committed his energies to this expensive work, with the peons, the helpers, and the material that the government gave him. The building cost him, however, without counting the value of these supplies, more than about 200 thousand pesetas (Ramirez 134)[17]; he would not have risked such enormous outlay without the guarantee of an irreversible authorization of the government that in all the periods of Carnival it could celebrate six public masked balls. The choice of the buildable area could not have been better; it compared favorably with the commercial center of Isabel II and the doors of Monserrate; it was located at the very animated center of the main paseo and in the angle of one of the main streets leading to the suburbs. When the building was completed, its interior was equal to those of the best coliseums in Europe and with a structure, capacity, and elegance very similar to those of the Teatro Real in Madrid, and the Liceo in Barcelona, but with the variations of ventilation currents and quality of seating that the climate required" (de la Pezuela 178).

While waiting for the Gran Teatro to be completed and to become the wonder of Havana, the enterprising and ingenious don Francisco Pancho Martí, who had been a building manager, turned himself into a theatrical manager in order to realize his

---

[17] "Its cost reached 400,000 pesos without counting the aid of workers and materials that General Tacón provided."

governor's great passion and had the enterprising idea of starting to put together a large troupe worthy of the undertaking. In the meantime, he used the two theaters he managed, the Principal and the Diorama, as a testing ground for such a troupe.

THEATERS OF L'ABANA

A. Coliseo or Principal Theater

It was not until 1773 that Havana had a permanent theater, when the Marquis de la Torre set out to raise the level of culture. The major comedies of Vega, Tirso, and Calderon were performed there by companies in transit or by amateurs in small buildings or makeshift halls or rooms.

Believing he was endowing the Casa de Recogidas, founded by Bishop Hechavarria, with a cultural foundation and offering the government a few pesetas from the seizure of Jesuit property, he created an association of notables for a public subscription to put together a theater of exclusive ownership. The proposal was successful and within four months resulted in "un modesto pero capaz teatro de mamposterla y tabla en un punto descubierto, llamado el Moninillo," at a cost of 35,800 pesetas. Don Bernardo Llagostera took charge of everything needed for the new theater. Just a thousand pesetas were enough to stage the weekly performances. Because of the war and the English domination between 1780 and 1783, in 1788 the theater was closed and lay in ruins for almost ten years, when the governor, Marquis de Somcruelos, completely restored it and the performances resumed. In the *Revista de Cuba*, D. Buenaventura Ferrer wrote: "Era de arquitectura magestuosa, y aunque de madera en su interior, estaba bien pintado y tenia buenas decoraciones," in that era "era el más hermoso teatro de la Monarquia" (Ramirez 22-23).

Other innovations came about at the beginning of 1846 with the good taste of Captain General Don Leopoldo O'Donnell, who decided to expand and embellish it with elegance and solidity with a fund of 30,000 pesetas. He entrusted the work to the engineer Mariano Carrillo de Albornoz, who planned to conclude it in December, "renovando con piedra silleria toda la fachada y costado de lla parte que mira al mar." He had been waiting impatiently for an Italian stone company coming from Genoa when on the night of October 10, 1846, the city was devastated by the horrendous storm.

O'Donnell undertook to rebuild, but insuperable difficulties were brought to his attention by the owner of the primitive building, the casa de San Juan Nepomuceno de Recogidas, and it was not decided whether to repair the building destroyed by the storm or to build a new one. The new captain, on behalf of Alcoy, opted for the repair, and he devised a lottery for construction, but everything took a long time, as his interest was not especially strong. In the municipal archives of Havana there is the record of a motion of the executive Joaquin Muños Izaguirre proposing the construction of a hotel or a mercantile center on the land of the theater. It was not until 1853 that the Junta, as an obligation of honor to the people in restoring the primitive theater intended for entertainment, appointed a commission for the purpose. Despite the sales of box seats, a request for aid to the government in February 1855, a loan from the Lyceum, had not come to any result. Subsequently, the ruined building and the adjoining land were put up for public auction in 1864 (de la Pezuela 177).

B. Diorama Theater

The Diorama was designed and built in 1827 by Juan Bautista Vermay (1786–1833), a painter and architect, but also a set designer, musician, and poet. Vermay was said to be a Freemason, who after wandering abroad after the fall of Napoleon in Italy, Germany, and the US, had settled in 1816 in Cuba

(Ramirez 128–133). Ferdinand VII, in consideration of the services rendered to the island, granted him the entire site of an industrial area for the construction of a theater, solid and elegant, which was called Diorama, some say because during the construction there was discovered a diorama depicting the cemetery of Father La Chaisse in Paris, others say because it served at the outset and for some time onward "para un espectàculo de vistas òpticas." It was inaugurated with an exhibition of drawings from the Free Academy of Painting and Drawing, a center of Cuban culture, and with the participation of well-known violists and other artists. A famous company was established there, those of the Spanish tragedian Andrés Prieto, and many other famous actors performed there.

On behalf of Captain General Don Francisco Dionisio Vives Vermay several commissions for paintings were done and he honored that island when many disciples placed on his tomb, on March 30, 1833, a highly laudatory epigraph of his qualities, which reads "Vermay reposa aquí. Su lumbre pura del entusiasmo iluminó su frente; un alma tuvo candida y ardiente, de artista el corazón y la ternura."

From 1842 the Diorama became the barracks and lodging of the commander of the "serenos" and was used for the public illumination system and therefore also as a storehouse for lights, costumes, and instruments. The famous hurricane of October 10, 1846 damaged it severely, and it was demolished on account of the heavy expenses that would have been involved for the restoration. Various buildings were built on the site.

C. Gran Teatro Tacón

In the same year, the Circo Habanera Theater, later called Teatro de Villanueva, was built. Miguel Tacón undertook to support the project through the purchase of construction materials, but he also helped supply laborers using the convicts of the Cárcel de La Habana, and he gave assistance in the form of advances of capital to be repaid with comfortable terms. Even with such use of convict labor it is said to have cost two hundred thousand pesos.

Marty became the builder, the manager, and in around 1857 the full owner, when with the deposit of 750 thousand pesetas he bought not only the main building, but also costumes, furniture, and decorations, along with land and various outbuildings. Most of the capital would be paid in installments and with the security that "los producttos de aquel gran coliseo, havrian de facilitar en poco anos el reintegro de la suma invertida en la compra y el de sus intereces."

After about six months of bureaucratic process, between the development of the projects, gaining approvals, and the setting up of the construction site, in August 1837 construction began under the direction of Antonio Mayo and the carpenter Miguel Nins y Pons.

The site was in some meadows beyond the fortified walls, making it part of an ambitious project of enhancing the area. The theater project therefore would be the driving force behind the enlargement of the city through urbanization, which would have resulted in a far-reaching use of capital for the resulting building speculation.

It stood on a level area of 3,315 varas (m 0.87 approximately) that would encompass the Porch, Vestibule, café, and Theater as part of the 6,176 square varas that was purchased from the Real Hacienda from July 1836 until 1839.

Construction was completed on February 28, 1838. And on Sunday, April 15, 1838, during the masked ball for the Carnival season, the solemn inauguration took place with the unveiling of the marble slab bearing the title "Gran Teatro de Tacón" in honor of the "provident and munificent" Capitan General de la Isla de Cuba, and with the staging of the five-act play *Don Juan de Austria or the Vocación* and a Bolero at the end, starring the famous Cuban actor Francisco Covarrubias. Each year four masked dances would take place, named Piñata, La Vieja, La Sardina, and Figurine.

In general, the press of the island agreed in recognizing the beauty and magnificence of the theater. Serafin Ramirez reports brilliant descriptions, beginning with de la Pezuela in his *Saggio storico di Cuba* (1866, 202): "Although modest on the outside, it equals, if not surpasses the major ones in Paris and London." This is what Nicolas Pardo Pimentel says in his *Manual of the Philharmonic*: "There are various theaters in the city of Havana, but the most spacious and magnificent is that of Tacón, situated in the center of the Alameda ... a simple shade or shutter divides the boxes from the corridors or galleries and in the front there is an elegant gilded iron grating that allows you to see from the hair down to the insolent foot of the graceful dame habaneras" (64). In her *Viaje á la Habana*, Santa Cruz y Montalvo writes: "This theater is rich and elegant, painted white and gold, the curtain and decorations offer such a brilliant point of view that it is impossible to observe it from any rule of perspective. The courtyard is filled with magnificent armchairs, the same as the boxes whose front has a light golden grating that allows the gaze of the curious to penetrate up to the feet of the spectators. Only the first theaters of the great capitals of Europe can match it in beauty of decoration and luxury of lighting and in the elegance of the spectators who all wear yellow gloves and white pants. In London or Paris, one would take this theater for an immense salon of great tone" (48).

Ramirez also transcribes the technical data taken from the *Revista Económica* no. 25 of May 1878: Stalls and stage occupied a space of 42.83 meters by 29, 69 m, and the widest part of the mouth measured 17.36 m. It had 56 boxes on the first and second floors, 8 on the third floor, 112 seats on the third floor, 500 seats in the auditorium, and the same number in the gallery for 2,287 spectators in addition to 750 standing behind the boxes, for a total of 3,037 people (Ramirez, 133–136).

Another description of the Tacón comes from José María de Andueza[18]: "Enter the theater through three gated doors that lead to a large courtyard, on whose sides there are two cafés, one for ice cream and one for wine; at the end of the side corridors of this courtyard and parallel to the previous ones, there are three more doors, through which you enter the

---

[18] Andueza (1809–1865), journalist, magazine contributor, and also theatrical writer, represented in Havana the drama *Guillermo* in 1838 and *Blanca de Navarra* in 1839 in the romantic style; he became governor of Toledo.

theater. Everything is luxurious in this: The boxes have an elegant view and allow, since they are open, that the beauties in them sit flaunting their rich costumes and ornaments, from their hairstyles to their short satin shoes."

The beautiful habaneras who frequented it were adorned in colorful dresses, the favorite colors being blue and white. They crowned their heads with a flower or a "Carey" comb. Others wore hats, a silk ribbon the same color as the silk of their shoes. Foreigners who visited were amazed to see those pretty habaneras, with small feet, eyes black or as blue as the tropical sky, with their long black hair in the form of a braid or loose and reaching to the waist.

Jacobo de la Pezuela complained that the grandeur of the hall and the proscenium, as was required in this class of buildings consecrated to the cult of entertainment and art, did not correspond to the solidity of the exterior architecture. Not a regular frontispiece, not a sculpture, nor the poorest relief embellish the monotonous facade of the great theater that was named for Tacón. The main entrance has an elegant portico with three arches in the façade, and one side boasts intermediate marble columns and three of relief on stonework in both corners.

To the right of the theater runs a low building facing the avenue where are located almost all the offices and workshops of the company. The discerning Marty had prepared by placing everything related to decoration, machinery, and carpentry immediately availing for his employees and very precise workers (de la Pezuela 178).

Situated today in front of Elizabeth II Mall, it was at the time the most splendid and opulent theater in the Americas, so much so that it was compared to La Scala in Milan and the Opéra National de Paris.

D. Artistic and Literary High School

In the years between 1840 and 1870, in this climate of cultural celebration in which music, both operatic and philharmonic, had become popular, there was a great impulse to create, and initiatives of all kinds were launched. Prominent companies of every order frequently visited the capital and encouraged the birth of artistic and cultural societies made up of both simple amateurs and artists of high rank.

In this spirit arose the famous Liceo Artistico y Literation, in that era "la más bella é interesante, la más útil y benéfica, la más rica en elementos de todas: clases la más generosa en sus propósitos, la más liberal en sus aspiraciones, y por último, la demás alto vuelo" (Ramirez 303-311; *Biblioteca* 7). The Liceo, unique in the island, in whose bosom were gathered the best minds and professors of first order, was founded and directed by don Ramón Pintó, "uno de esos hombres cúyo claro talento, espíritu creador, firme, incansable y de elevadas mirais, de entusiasmo inagotable, con íntimas y extensas relaciones, habría sidocapaz de llevarla aún más allá del altísimo grado de prestigio y esplendor en que la habia colocado" (Ramirez, 304).

The Liceo's inauguration took place on the night of October 19, 1844. The greatest share of the event was the performance of Vincenzo Bellini's *Norma*, which had been performed for the 1832 Carnival and Lent season at La Scala on December 26, 1831. This was followed by a duet from Rossini's *Semiramide* (La Fenice in Venice, February 3, 1823), a "galopada cromatica de Liszt." Ramón Gazque had great success singing the aria of Pollione. The school was divided into five sections: sciences, literature, fine arts, music, and declamation. The honorary president was the Captain General, and it was self-supporting with members' dues of between 450 and 500 pesetas and with income from hosting ballroom dancing. The weekly activities were strictly theatrical, both dramatic and operatic, as well as artistic and literary, sometimes involving painting exhibitions, floral games, and prizes. Every year Gioachino Rossini's *Stabat* was performed with orchestra and choir, as well as *Norma*, Gaetano Donizetti's *Ana Bolena* (premiered at Teatro Carcano in Milan, December 26, 1830) and *Lucia di Lammermoor* (premiered at San Carlo in Naples, September 26, 1835), and Vincenzo Bellini's *Sonnambula* (Teatro Carcano, March 6, 1831) and his *Puritani* (Paris, January 24, 1835). With donations from the 800 subscribing members, the Liceo daily increased its rich library and held sixteen classes of studies in which the twenty-two most accredited professors of the island taught free of charge the French and English languages, physics, fencing, hygiene, Greek, literature, natural history, flute and oboe, piano, psychology, and painting, with attendance of up to 295 pupils. It supported artists and carried out charitable and patriotic activities. The Liceo also dedicated itself to the promotion of letters and the arts on the island through its weekly magazine, published since 1856, *Liceo de la Habana*. As of December 31, 1857, it had assets of 1,564,599 pesetas (de la Pezuela 177–178; Ramirez 303–311).

The Liceo increased its importance in this year when it bought the great Tacón Theater from Francisco Marty for 750,000 pesetas, which included not only the main building, but also the warehouses of clothing, sets, and decorations and the land and outbuildings he had acquired during the twenty-seven years of ownership. Marty held a considerable number of shares in the Liceo's limited company. It was not difficult for the theater to become Marty's property again (de la Pezuela 177–178; Ramirez 303–311).

The Italian Theatre Company

As impresario of the only large and most important Teatro Principal, Marty felt that he could enlist an Italian troupe and have them debut and perform for a few seasons in this theater while waiting for the dream of a lifetime, the Gran Teatro, to be completed.

And what troupe could have been better than an excellent and close-knit Italian group? Those were the years in which Italian opera was at the height of its splendor throughout the world, and many impresarios sought operatic works for company engagements. For Marty, the Teatro La Pergola troupe was the one that could fulfill his expectations in terms of quality and professionalism.

To compete with the best European theaters, according to Tacón's ambitions, Marty made things big and enlisted for very ambitious show projects a full troupe, from the great interpreters to the simple workers. He signed a lavish five-year contract with seventy-nine fellow professionals of different roles to cover the entire theatrical staff, no one excluded, from singers to dancers, choristers, orchestral soloists, extras, and finally the simple and low-level laborers, technicians, workers, janitors, seamstresses, and secretaries. It was a complete Teatro Stabile.

It so happened that during the assembly of this grandiose troupe Marty went to Florence and contacted the artists and workers of La Pergola. Among these enlisted there were Antonio Meucci as "engineer, stagehand and designer," and his wife Ester Mochi as costume designer, "director of tailoring" of the theater. Apartments for the workers were provided for housing. For Meucci, who had up to that point lived an unfortunate and miserable existence and was a frequent guest of his homeland jails, this was a miracle, one of those that happen not to many and not often in the course of life. He had never dreamed he would leave Florence, where his name in the penal files left him with few prospects of freedom or appreciable hopes of a dignified job. Given the limited horizons of the Grand Duchy, a new and far more dangerous and serious problem were his now-confirmed Mazzinian beliefs. The Grand Duke was not as enlightened as some patriotic propaganda would have us believe. And with his record Meucci could only dream of traveling to foreign countries. And similar occupational or political climates were all that could have been found in the provincial states of Italy in that era.

The decision to emigrate at the time might have seemed crazy and adventurous, especially going to a land that was, to that point, outside the usual migratory circuits of Italians. Safe havens and the support of many fellow countrymen could be found first and foremost in the United States, with a strong block of fellow countrymen, and also in Argentina. But in his Florentine experiences, in his libertarian spirit, as well as in his experimental techniques in the mysterious and complex world of nature, the enterprising Meucci did not fear. With this spirit, the couple found in Cuba the right place, a great family of close-knit artists, and an open welcome. They found their safe place of peace and happiness, sheltered from economic problems for the next fifteen years. With the five-year contract, Meucci had a workshop where he could make theatrical equipment.

They embarked as stowaways at the port of Livorno on the Sardinian ship *Coccodrillo*, which transported goods rented from the manager and adapted on that occasion for passengers. No passport was needed for passengers who were not supposed to be there. Meucci was turning his back on his hometown, a departure with no return. The *Journal of Commerce* of the Port-Franco of Livorno of October 7, 1835, listed the departure on the fifth without mentioning eighty-one passengers who instead were noted in the newspaper *El Noticioso y Lucero* of Havana of December 17, 1835: "Puerto de la habana entradas de ayer De Liorna en 72 días, 81 individuos de la compañia De ópoera italiana para esta ciudad." A ship with a cargo of men and tons of stage props making it to Cuba in seventy-two days of sailing is a kind of miracle.

Just two months after arriving in Havana, in February 1836 Pancho Martí, by now familiar with the scope of the important business he had undertaken, told Meucci: "His Excellency the Governor has received authorization from Madrid and today I have signed the contract that commits me to build and run the new theater in the zone of extramuros. The theater will be operational in two years, in time for the temporada de Bailes de Carnaval. As for the stage and all the equipment, I trust only you, Señor Meucci. You have carte blanche and will take orders only from me."

The architectural works of the Gran Teatro, the most luxurious of its time, were completed in 1838, and the Meuccis moved into the employees' quarters, where they had their workshops, a workshop for the tools and machinery of the theater, and one for theatrical tailoring.

Meucci became general director for maintenance, restoration, and modernization of works. He installed gas lighting throughout the building and invented a revolutionary ventilation system in 1847, following the serious damage suffered by the theater during a hurricane. This was necessary due to the city's climate and avoided the danger of the roof blowing off. He created toilets for women, something never seen before in a Latin American theater. After these technical-structural interventions, in order to guarantee better usability of the theater, he moved on to the strictly technical solutions of functionality and management and utility of the stage instruments for the shows. He brought from the United States modern and innovative machinery that would make it possible to raise and lower the stage floor in a few seconds. He came up with an innovative complex of curtains, which he made safer with the adoption of a firebreak. It was his knowledge of engineering and chemistry that gave him opportunities, previously unthinkable for an unknown immigrant, to design a modern and luxurious stage. This experience would be used in his long future career in the service of the theater, especially after the redesign of the theater building, half destroyed by terrible hurricane, a catastrophe that will remain forever in the collective memory of Cubans.

This same professional experience as an engineer and chemist was useful to him in creating a water purification system at the Gran Teatro de Tacón, not only to make it drinkable but also to feed a system of fountains.

As technical director of the theater he diverted the underground course of a river that flowed nearby to create a resonance chamber that significantly improved the building's acoustics. It is said that when his successors closed the theater, a soprano, having experienced that the acoustics had worsened, protested and begged that it be reopened. Basilio Catania (1926–2010) passed along this story and reported the testimony of a Nestor Baguer, who boasted ancestors who co-owned the theater with Francisco Marty and who knew many anecdotes about Meucci's abilities that had been handed down to him.

Meucci also created works outside of his theater commitments. Don Manuel Pastor, chief technical and mechanical engineer and inspector of fortifications, faced serious difficulty with the potability of the water in the new Fernando VII aqueduct he had built. It was Meucci who, between 1835 and 1840, solved the problems related to the hardness of the water and provided chemical purification of traces of pollutants that could not be eliminated with mechanical filters. He also advised methodical analyses and calibrated additions of substances such as soda. Today the purification procedures are more complex and involve a wide range of chemicals, the most common being chlorine for transformation into sodium hypochlorite. The same lines of research and implementation were adopted for a filtering system for tea and coffee.

Meucci's knowledge of chemistry provided ingenious solutions for those times, including possible commercial and economic ones. One of these was a method of preservation of corpses, an unusual matter, but one that could be commercially profitable because of the prospect of fulfilling the desire of immigrants to send back home the bodies of relatives in good condition. However, the cost of equipment and material prevented the success of this among many of his brilliant inventions.

At the beginning of 1842 he became involved in studies of galvanostegy, a method of electrolytic coverage, which had been discovered in 1791 by Luigi Galvani and perfected by Johann Wilhelm Ritter in 1800, and which used a current produced by a voltaic pile.

Luigi Galvani (1737–1798), who had degrees in medicine and in philosophy and who was professor of anatomy and obstetrics at the Academy of Sciences and the University of Bologna (1769–1797), devoted himself to research after being dismissed for refusing to swear allegiance to the Cisalpine Republic. He went on to study the forces of electricity in muscular motion (*De viribus electricitatis in motu muscolari*, 1701); this is the theory that was called "galvanism." Applications of this ranged from physical and chemical methodologies in the study of organisms at the beginning of the eighteenth century to the therapeutic use of electricity in the middle of the century and solutions formulated by Isaac Newton of "affinity" or "identity" between what physicists called "electrical flux" and what physiologists called "nervous fluid." Galvani wanted to show that the "animal spirits" of ancient physiology were the effects of hidden electricity in the nerves, which had similar or coincident characteristics with those of common electricity. Alessandro Volta voiced some criticisms, and Galvani's experiments were partially abandoned. It was Berlin physiologist Emil Du Bois Reymond (1818–1896) who founded electrophysiology among the biological sciences and demonstrated with new experiments an electricity specific to animals. This function of Volta's conductors of electricity explained the famous contractions observed by Galvani in the frog experiment. He expressed in this way his absolute pessimism about the attempts to unveil the mysteries of the universe, such as the origin of life, free will, essence of force and matter: *Ignoramus et ignorabimus*, "we ignore them, and we will ignore them."

Galvani's studies were continued by his nephew Giovanni Aldini (1762–1834) at the University of Bologna (1798–1807), whom Meucci must certainly have known. It was he who spread the discoveries about animal electricity at a popular level and studied its medical and technical applications, such as the construction and illumination of lighthouses.

In 1840 the Swiss Auguste de la Rive had realized the method of gilding silver and brass, for which he was given a prize by the French Academy of Sciences. Albert Sorel in 1937 had used the term *galvanization* and obtained patents for hot-dip galvanizing. The practice covered many applications such as chrome plating, nickel plating, and gold plating. This was profitable for Meucci in October 1843, when the new Spanish governor Leopold O'Donnell signed a four-year contract with him, the first in the Americas, to galvanize army supplies and private items. The contract expired on February 1, 1848, and Meucci was left with only electroplating, the galvanizing of private individuals' objects.

As a result of the research and discoveries that he was making, Meucci enjoyed prestige and success such that on December 16, 1844, he was given an evening of honor at the Grand Theater of Tacón and was entrusted with the direction of work on its renovation following damage caused by a violent hurricane. He was also said to have helped finance the insurgents of the 1848 revolution.

THE TELETROPHONE IN HAVANA

Already in 1835 at the Tacón Theater, in order to facilitate communications and to give orders to the stagehands, Meucci had modified the Florentine project of the primitive corded mouthpiece stretched between two funnels on a parchment membrane. He devised the idea of transmitting at a distance the vibrations of the membrane of an acoustic cornet by means of electric current, thereby, as he said, "telegraphing the word" (Respighi 19).

In 1846 he had designed and built a device for electrotherapy with excellent results. It was equipped with a pulse generator (lasting about 1 minute) with a rotating cross, anticipating the criteria adopted in modern commercial instruments. Because of his research and experiments into electrotherapy in 1849 he discovered the transmission of the voice by electrical means, the first time in history, which he called a "talking telegraph" and later, a "teleptophone."

But his creative impulses found another field of investigation—Mesmer's electrical therapeutic systems, which some doctors proposed that he employ to experiment on patients suffering from rheumatism. Amazed by the physiological responses of the human body to the stimuli of the "electro-medicine" (today's magnetotherapy, which was already being practiced in Europe and America), he began experiments on the use of short electrical pulses for the treatment of pain.

The most revolutionary discoveries in the scientific field often occur by chance, when one deviates from established canons or thoroughly disregards scientific protocols, or when one disregards established tradition. Thus, Isaac Newton's tree and apple in that *annus mirabilis* 1666. Voltaire, in the fifteenth of his *Lettres philosophiques* (1734), stated that it was upon seeing this phenomenon that Newton understood why the Moon did not fall to Earth like the apple.[19] In fact, the legend was promoted by a contemporary writer, William Stukeley, who reported in his *Memoirs of Sir Isaac Newton's Life* a conversation of April 5, 1726, in Kensington, in which Newton recalled "when formerly, the notion of gravitation came into his mind. 'why should that apple always descend perpendicularly to the ground,' thought he to him self: occasion'd by the fall of an apple, as he sat in a comtemplative mood: 'why should it not go sideways, or upwards? but constantly to the earths centre?'" (Stukeley 15). This extraordinary event had a precedent in the third century BCE with Archimedes's tank and his cry "èureka," "I have found, when he discovered hydrostatics or "floating bodies."

---

[19] See his *Lettres philosophiques*, "Quinziènne lettre, Sur le système de l'attraction": "S'étant retiré en 1666 à la campagne, près de Cambridge, un jour qu'il se promenait dans son jardin et qu'il voyait des fruits tomber d'un arbre, il se laissa aller à une méditation profonde sur cette pesanteur dont tous les philosophes ont cherché si longtemps la cause en vain, et dans laquelle le vulgaire ne soupçonne pas de mystère... Mais, si la lune obéit à ce principe, quel qu'il soit, n'est-il pas encore très raisonnable de croire que les autres planètes y sont également soumises ?"

Meucci's discoveries related to the transmission of sound through a wire began when a man suffering from migraines came to him. Placing a small copper electrode on the patient's tongue and on his own, he sent a mild electric shock to the patient, who signaled the effect with a cry of surprise. He thus discovered the "electrophonic" effect, the phenomenon later known as "physiophony." The man thanked him and left cured of his migraine. Meucci repeatedly demonstrated the physiophonic phenomenon, always eliciting surprise in patients. It was the first step toward the transmission of voice and the test of the telephone system in 1849, when Alexander Graham Bell, born in Edinburgh on March 3, 1847, was only two years old.

This would be Meucci's good fortune and an experiment that would change his life. Let's read what he himself recounted during the famous Bell/Globe trial:

> Having read Mesmer's treatise on animal magnetism, I got the idea of applying and experimenting with it, applying electricity to sick people by order of some doctor friend who ... didn't have much to do so he also suggested that I give shocks to several people who were employed by me—Negroes—and sometimes to my spouse; at the same time I had moved from my laboratory to a third room an electric conductor and produced electricity for a series of Bunsen batteries that he kept in my laboratory.
>
> One day [about 1849] there came a person known to me who was ill with rheumatism of the head. I placed him in the third room, I put in his hand the two conductors that communicated with the battery, which at the end of said conductors held a tool, isolated from the conductor, made of cork, of the form that I describe here; above this cork a metal tab soldered to the conductor of insulated copper wire passed through the interior of said cork and communicated with the battery. In my laboratory, where I held an instrument equal to the one he held in his hand, I ordered him to put the metal tongue in his mouth so

that, being in communication with me of the electric fluid, he would want to know where his disease was. I put the same tool to my ear. At the moment when the sick person put the tongue to his lips he received a discharge and gave a scream. At the same moment I heard a sound. I stopped the operation, and in order to prevent the case of the electric shock that the person had received, I had the idea of remedying that case. I took the two utensils, the one that the person held in his hand and the one I held in mine, and I lined them with a cardboard wrapper so as to insulate the tongue from contact with the flesh; I ordered the sick person to repeat the operation done previously, not to have any fear of being more hurt by the electricity and also to speak freely inside the wrapper. He did it immediately. He put his wrapper to his mouth and I put mine to my ear. At the moment that the aforesaid individual spoke I received the sound of the word, not distinct, a murmur, an inarticulate sound. I repeated several times in the same day. Then I tried again on different days and got the same result. From this moment it was my imagination and I recognized that I had obtained the transmission of human speech by means of conductive wire joined with several batteries to produce electricity, to which I immediately gave the name of "Talking Telegraph." This was about the end of '49 to '50. ... I ceased my experiments on said object, reserving them for my arrival in New York, for which I had to leave Havana from '50 to '51. I had an immense number of batteries, about 60.[20]

Thus ended the exhilarating experience of Havana, but it was less exhilarating for the theater, which at the beginning of the twentieth century saw all of Meucci's workshops and adjoining buildings demolished to make way for the construction of the Centro Gallego, a monumental and ambitious social headquarters for Galician immigrants designed by Belgian Paul Belau

---

[20] U.S. Circuit Court, Southern District of New York, pp. 214 and pp. 108 of appendices and pp. 111 of English translation of 61 publications on Bourseul and Reis. Copy in the New York Public Library.

and the firm of Purdy and Henderson and inaugurated in 1915 incorporating the hall and stage of the Gran Teatro de Tacón. Only after the Revolution of Fidel Castro and Che Guevara would the Galician halls of the old Tacón be converted into rehearsal and studio rooms for the Ballet Nacional de Cuba and other performing arts activities. In 2016 the original stage and main hall, after a radical round of restoration and modernization, was named Gran Teatro de La Habana "Alicia Alonso," in homage to Cuba's greatest artist. The current Gran Teatro Colón grew up around the old (Bonvía).

Chapter 4

The Gamble of New York

Since December 17, 1835, some fifteen years of theatrical work and experiments had passed. The Florentine was famous in the city and esteemed for his heterodox and extraordinary qualities. The Meuccis had become rich and landed in April 1850 in New York on the frigate *Norma*, bringing with them Antonio's laboratory supplies and a handsome fortune of no less than twenty-six thousand pesos fuertes (about $500,000), their life savings.

Once again, he found himself without stable employment after the third expiration of his contract with Don Francisco. But the matter was more complicated: The impresario's government concession for the exclusive management of theatrical performances in Havana had also expired. For Meucci, the fame of his electrical experiments must have influenced his decision to leave, and his friends advised him to move to America, the most propitious place for the implementation and commercialization of his discoveries. And New York City was the city that was beginning to become the capital of gambling. The fear that the governor was aware of his political ideas and help given to Garibaldi is said to have played a role in the decision. The impresario and his family and his entire company left on March 23, 1850, for Charleston. Meucci did not even think about returning to Italy and the Florence of the Grand Duke, as would have seemed natural and logical. The mirage, the promised land, appeared to be the United States.

For the impresario it was a promising choice for a country that was beginning to open up to opera and offered great opportunities for those who wanted to organize opera performances. Mozart's legendary librettist (*Le nozze di Figaro*, *Don Giovanni*, *Così fan tutte*), the Venetian adventurer Lorenzo Da Ponte (1749–1838), had landed at the age of fifty-six in New York and worked first as a grocer, then bookseller. He spent time between Philadelphia and New York City, and he returned several times to Italy. In addition to opening a boarding school (Ann Da Ponte's Boarding House) in 1821, he inaugurated a school of Italian at Columbia University, created for him in 1825 by Clement Moore, which would become the glorious Casa Italiana during the Fascist era. On the musical side, in addition to staging *Don Giovanni* at the Park Theatre, he was the first to present Rossini's *Il barbiere di Siviglia* in the US. At eighty years old, he promoted a tour of his granddaughter Giulia, who in 1830 performed his opera *L'ape musicale* with little success. In the promotion of Italian opera, great importance was given to the invitation to the patriot Piero Maroncelli who accepted and moved, along with his wife, Amalia Schneider. Da Ponte, by now a naturalized citizen, in 1833 founded his own Italian Opera House, which was inaugurated with Rossini's *La gazza ladra*, but which however failed after two years due to deficit and was finally destroyed by fire.

So, the group's paths diverged after fifteen years of common work, a period of life lived together in the glories and new experiences of a new world for them. Meucci delayed his departure due to the death of his only daughter, as can be seen from the obituary in *The Sun* of October 19, 1889: "In 1850 Meucci came to New York from Cuba, where his only child, a girl of 6, had just died." Meucci may have suffered from some type of sterility, possibly a consequence of a severe form of syphilis contracted at age twenty-one. The *Diario de la Marina* announced the departure for Sunday, April 7, 1850, but the departure of the American ship *Norma*, fixed at first for April 16, actually took place Tuesday, April 23, 1850. His wife Ester was leaving that humid climate that was harmful to her rheumatism. According to the biographer Catania, some passengers during the crossing felt immense fear at the strong south-westerly winds, and to take their minds off it the boatswain Nando, a true Neapolitan, burst into a Punchinello-style performance, hopping about with his arms folded at his sides while singing "E vvuie lasciatevi dondolàare" to the passengers.

On May 1, 1850, they landed in New York and settled in Clifton, a neighborhood in Staten Island. Marty had reached Richmond, and here his path intersected with that of Max Maretzek, who was well acquainted with Marty's character and also with his activities as a great and appreciated impresario of the opera house in Havana.

As for Marty, Maretzek wrote:

> As, however, it would have been difficult to procure available singers from Italy, and well-nigh impossible to lure artists of decided merit to Havana for the few winter months, Señor Marti was obliged to engage his company for a much longer period. And as during the intervals they could not remain in Cuba, in consequence of the great heat and the fears of the yellow fever, for two years he used to send them to New York. Here they played in Castle Garden, once a fort, afterwards an opera house and now the dépôt for emigrants from Europe. While his artists were no better than those we had in New York, this concurrence was of no import to the interests of the New York management. In the summer of 1850, however, Marti sent to this city the greatest troupe which had ever been heard in America. Indeed, in point of the integral talent, number, and excellence of the artists composing it, it must be admitted that it has seldom been excelled in any part of the Old World.

After listing the cast and the great European references, he added, in a letter to Joseph Fischof: "This company not only created a profound sensation in New York but played for something less than half the usual price. The admission to Castle Garden, during their performances, was no more than fifty cents" (Maretzek 1855, 155–157).

But it was during a difficult financial situation and amid disagreements within his company that he witnessed Marty's arrogance and power. He had been his agent in Richmond, involved in controversy with the press and also in serious trouble with singers placed under his charge in Charleston, who had roughed him up. Maretzek writes:

> Now, although the artists who had placed themselves in this difficulty by an open act of rebellion deserved no pity at my hands, there were many, in this instance, innocent subalterns (members of the Orchestra, Chorus, and other officials) connected with or engaged in the Southern division of my company, whom I could not conscientiously allow to remain in a strange city without the means either of return or of subsistence. It was true that I had had a good season in New York, but the profits had been swallowed up by the outstanding debts of my preceding musical campaign. What, then, was I to do? The immediate necessity for action forced me to take the readiest means of assisting them that was in my power, and I was consequently obliged to sacrifice the greatest portion of my operatic stock, music, dresses, and properties, to enable myself to bring back to New York the headless and tailless company who were amusing themselves as best they could in the city of Savannah. (Maretzek 197–198)

He was willing to make sacrifices, but he had to deal with jealousies and, above all, with disputes with impresarios in order to grab the top Italian companies. Therefore,

> Now, in making this sacrifice, it had been my intention to unite all my musical forces here, with the purpose of starting with the whole of them, by another *route*, under my own command.
> This intention was unhappily doomed not to be put into

execution. Some other of those musical agents who had lately so plentifully cropped up out of the manure Barnum had spread upon the soil of American humanity, had recently become aware of my somewhat precarious position. Representing themselves, whether rightly or wrongly, it would be impossible to say (the word of a musical agent can never be taken without doubt) as employed by Marty, the Havanese *impressario*, they began to disseminate discord in my company. (Maretzek 198)

He continues:

> These gentlemen (if I am not wrong in giving them such a name) intimated to the members of it that Don Francisco had the intention of engaging them again for Havana, with the view of sending them, after the season for Opera in that city had terminated, to New Orleans, and thence to Mexico. If, however, they should determine upon accompanying me to New Orleans, Marty would certainly not engage them, as their novelty on one portion of the ground selected for his later musical campaign would clearly be destroyed. Therefore, in visiting that city with me, they would throw away the probability of obtaining an engagement of some eighteen or twenty-four months with him. These inventions were naturally listened to, and more foolishly believed. They thought it better to sacrifice their certain two or three months with me (they were still engaged for this period) than to risk the mere probability of a two years' engagement with Marty.
>
> Having made up their minds, therefore, to this course, they not only refused to proceed with me to New Orleans but announced their intention of definitely breaking their present engagement.
>
> Knowing my reduced means, they leagued themselves with the view of performing on their own account, until Marti should think proper to offer to re-engage them.
>
> But the internal jealousies and dissensions which exist in every Opera *troupe* did not permit them fully and completely to carry out this plan.

This is where the likes and dislikes of the prima donnas came into play. The great soprano Miss Steffanone was disliked by Bosio; Beneventano hated Cesare Badiali. "If there was any of the company whom Salvi specially disliked and mistrusted, it was Signor Bettini." With these singers he was ready to start a season in New Orleans, while others created their own Union Italian Opera Company that "waited to receive a proposition from Don Francisco Marty y Torrens" (Maretzek 198-200).

In this context of great companies and operatic performances, what is surprising is the proposition even then of the "diva," which we attribute in more recent times to film actresses, a title that certainly better suited the divine excellence of the sopranos of the times. This is how Maretzek widely described them:

> Operatic divinities are exclusively of the feminine sex, and therefore are usually called "divas," and like the ancient Grecian goddesses are divided into divas and demi-divas, according to their positions in the legitimate opera, or the bouffe-opera. But one undisputed fact remains in all their biographies: the graces surrounded their cradles from the moment of their birth; Venus bathed them in the bloom of youth and Cupid fanned the flies away from their little dimpled faces. The demi-divas, as the opera-bouffe prima donnas are called, are usually distinguished from the legitimate divas by an entire absence of voice. They sing with their feet, make shakes with their heads, arpeggios and chromatic scales with their hands, gruppettos with their eyes, cadenzas with an undulating movement of their body, and their talent and strength lies just there where the vulnerable spot of Siegfried in the Nibelungen is located. All divas and demi-divas with a few exceptions are enchanting at a distance, when viewed through an opera glass, but if you would know them as near as I do, you would soon realize that they are no more real stars than those painted on any theatrical scenery; that the crowns those queens of song wear are only pasteboard

or gilded tin , and that they are only divas or "Goddesses" of an Ingersollian type, id est: as long as their impresarios find it to their interest to pay for advertising them as such. (Maretzek 1890, 1–2)

To conclude, in this web of encounters and disagreements between Marty and the host, how and why did Meucci not have the possibility to continue his activity and only had the trivial consolation of living in the cottage of a great impresario, musician, and opera director like Max Maretzek? For these questions we find no answers, and we cannot but remain sad for the many things we do not know and wonder about why.

Of Meucci, Maretzek writes, "Natives of Florence, the Meuccis had spent fifteen years in Havana. Lorenzo Salvi, tenor with the Havana Company, lived in a Staten Island house with them briefly, as did Giuseppe Garibaldi, the Italian patriot who helped unify Italy. Meucci, an inventor, also ran a candle-making business" ((Maretzek 2006, 19).

THE ABODE OF LIFE

The climate of solidarity and friendship found and experienced for years in Cuba was treated differently in New York, where the old establishment, rooted and stable, felt a certain mistrust toward the new immigrants and exhibited that sense of fear and even hostility that is still found today toward "foreigners" in all societies around the globe. It was the feeling of mistrust and the fear of losing acquired privileges, the fear of being deprived of something strictly personal, one's own. It was and is the possible threat to their social class, from the middle class, a common and irrational case, from the previous, earlier immigrants. Hence the restrictive immigration legislation that was being experimented with, involving selection of potential immigrants by health criteria, but also with fears of terrorism, then identified with anarchy, looming invoking the unforgettable and eternal symbols of Sacco and Vanzetti. Once immigrants had passed the harsh tests, enduring racist encounters, a kind of Caudine Forks of Ellis Island, they were left in the hands of relatives who had come for them, or abandoned to the traffic of poorly paid or illegal labor, often handed over to the organized underworld. Much recent filmography has presented the vicissitudes of the Italians, often horrific and tragic, that a certain culture has propounded to us, with the Italian "padrino" and mafioso images. They experienced the difficulty of fitting in fully in that society on a par with Anglo-Saxons and relegation to certain ghettoized neighborhoods. Little Italy was an identity, but also a ghetto much like the ghettos of Jewish memory in Europe.

As a result, the Meuccis' residence in Clifton and then Rosebank, the Staten Island neighborhood where they lived for the rest of their lives, was not easy.

They bought a cottage, that typical four-room wooden house, built in 1840, the same one that houses today's Museum, and also a piece of land and had to come up with a new business. If in Havana they had arrived with a contract and a prestigious job, here on this island, in the true sense of the word, the Meucci family had taken a leap in the dark. Everything rested on the nice nest egg earned in Cuba, a solid base, but one that could not have lasted forever without a stable job, a decent occupation. And yet the Meucci family arrived with a professionalism consolidated by years of work and improvements, with genius and inventions still to come that opened up revolutionary scenarios and others in the making, the incessant research impulse that in Meucci was never exhausted.

On the land he built the small factory for candles produced of his invention with a smokeless formula with which he tried to start a solid business, hiring Italian immigrants and hoping to sell and have a substantial income from the sale to neighbors, parishes, and shopkeepers. Ester, as a great theatrical costume designer, adapted and contributed with her work as a seamstress for the neighbors and the demands of the place.

What is hard to understand is how he missed the opportunity to continue the profession that had given him so much glory from the Pergola to the Colón, theater work. Here there were no opportunities. Yet opera was all the rage in New York with the opening of new theaters and the great success of touring companies. It was a magical moment for opera and certainly for Italian companies and singers.

It is even stranger that his friendship with the tenor Lorenzo Salvi (Ancona 1810–Bologna 1879) had no effect. After his glorious experiences at La Scala in 1839 and his acclaimed presence in various theaters in Italy (Rome, Padua) and abroad (Vienna, Paris, London, St. Petersburg, Warsaw, Moscow, Madrid), Salvi had sung in the Havana Opera Company of Francisco Martí y Torrens when Meucci was stage designer at Tacón. In 1850 he made his debut in New York, where he made an impression on the scene of the city for "the splendid resonance, the vigor of the declamation, the tragic sadness of the expression" but he also became known for blackmailing relations with impresarios and an overbearing attitude toward the public. He contributed "to the purchase of the land on which Meucci's candle factory in Staten Island was built: the company became a center for the collection of Italian exiles, and Garibaldi also worked there, who in his letters to Salvi's brother-in-law, Eliodoro Spech, alludes with affection to the tenor from Marche" (Landini).[21] Eliodoro Spech, son of opera

---

[21] Landini cites the opinion in 1853 of the critic William Henry Fry, in Lawrence (343). He also reports that in RAI's 1970 three-part television miniseries, *Antonio Meucci cittadino toscano contro il monopolio Bell* Salvi appeared singing *Verranno a te*

singers and a famous tenor himself, also fought in Rome in 1849 and was in regular correspondence with Garibaldi; he too had been in Cuba and, living for a long time in the USA, in 1855 he obtained American citizenship, but he preferred to interrupt his career at the age of forty-six and return home (DeSantis). And did knowing Spech and Spech's excellent position not help Meucci? What prevented the leap, the continuation of his activity? Wouldn't a report of his exceptional talents as a stage designer and theatrical engineer performed for so many years in the sublime Tacón have sufficed?

Here, in this second part of his life, in the New York of sure affirmations and great prospects, everything will go wrong for Meucci. The stupendous life of glories and successes of the Pergola and the Tacón theaters ended forever. Was it just bad luck? Was it due to mistaken initiatives? Certainly, he was the victim of intrigue and of the incompetence of the American legal system. Once Ester died, the last five years of his life will be lived in obscurity, solitude, and poverty.

The letter sent to his brother Giuseppe, hospitalized in S. Maria Nuova in Florence, on November 14, 1855, indicates this desolation and discouragement in the New York of opportunities: "If I don't write to you more, I do it not to give you more pain than you have, because I can't tell you anything else except that I am in very bad circumstances and perhaps need to escape and go elsewhere. I have finished everything I had, and I have nothing left but the house and the land and the factory where the candles were made. But it is useless to talk about these now, they are not to be found for sale. Now I've started making pianos, but that's no good either. So, you can see that for me there is no luck and everything I undertake does not suit me. Believe me: In the degree in which I am I would rather

---

sull'aure from *Lucia di Lammermoor* with the voices of Giuseppe Di Stefano and Maria Callas.

be at home in the midst of misery and cholera than stay here."
In 1865, the property was sold by the local sheriff to a brewer (Respighi 21–22).

FACTORIES
The Sausage Factory

Daily life is demanding for everyone, whatever the degree of fame and genius of the person. Even for a refugee hero and waiting for subsidies the question of food imposed itself with its vulgar demands and even Garibaldi, a famous man but without work, had to get busy. None of his many admirers could offer to support him, as they were still refugees themselves.

The two men thought of starting production of salami and began with the simplest system in a small hut to make sausages. An expert in this field and perhaps the prompter of the enterprise was the Bologna native Major Bovi Campeggi (1814–1874), the unfailing and omnipresent shadow of the general who will follow in the Expedition of the Thousand. In his diary, Garibaldi wrote about regretting all the companions he had to leave behind in Africa: "And when I decided to go to America, my means did not allow me to take all my companions with me, so I left Leggiero and Coccelli in Tangier with my recommendation, and I chose Bovi to accompany me, who was unable to work because he was missing his right hand" (Garibaldi 266).

Imagine Garibaldi, using a sharp knife, cutting the meat from the bones, and mincing it. Even a butcher needs years of apprenticeship and experience. It happened that in his haste, his cutting hand did not distinguish between a slice of meat and a fingertip, which ended up being minced together with the meat. Everyone tried to look for the piece of finger, but it is said that Garibaldi reassured them: "Forget it, it's going to knead with sausages and we're going to eat Republican salami." There must have been several reasons for the company's failure. What is certain is that Bolognese industry and tastes did not take root among emigrants and islanders, so they had to get rid of their merchandise quickly. The island's market must not have been so robust among poor people who counted their pennies. Certainly, no rich vacationer could follow their Bolognese tastes. It was the first of the series of failures that would accompany the pair and would continue up until the end of Meucci's life.

The Candle Factory

Meucci was back to square one, with no money and no prospects. This time the general wanted to bet on the genius of the engineer set designer, always busy in his modest laboratory experimenting with something. And he was experimenting with something new, always in his familiar field of chemistry. At this time, when he didn't know that electricity could produce light; it was obtained by means of the flame that illuminated. From the lights of the caves, after the theft of the fire of Prometheus, it had passed to the oil lamps. Terracotta containers ranging from the simplest forms, such as a flat container with a spout and a wick, to the most whimsical or artistic, such as figurative lamps, were all oil lamps, as oil was the most common material.

Thus, Homer introduces us even to Pallas Athena, who, "ahead with a golden lamp, made a beautiful light" (*Odyssey* XIX, 33–34). This was also the custom in Cnossos of Crete. Certainly, the smoke was annoying and some of Meucci's forerunners tried to remedy this, such as Gerolamo Cardano (1501–1576) with his special tank that regulated the oil's flow, or the ingenious Aimé Argant with his burner, invented in 1783, with the wick in the form of a ribbon between two cylinders that reduced smoke and increased luminosity.

Now Meucci had invented another method. Already by 1818 he had begun to use stearin or tristearina, a triglyceride (due to the condensation of stearic acid and glycerol), in making his candles. Unlike wax it did not drip. Meucci used instead a new formula, which was kerosene, a waxy mass, whitish, insoluble in water and that is a mixture of solid hydrocarbons obtained from petroleum and that was produced for the first time by the German industrialist Karl von Reichdenback in 1830.

It's not that things were going well with all these ventures. In a letter to his brother dated December 20, 1859, he wrote: "I am obliged to work in a candle factory in my old age like a black man and at only 15 scudi a week, a day that is given to a porter here, and to live I am obliged to do this" (Respighi 71).

Garibaldi made no mention of the sausage experiment in his memoirs. He gave the memoirs to Theodore Dwight (1796–1866), writer of diaries and tourist guides and a supporter between 1850 and 1860 of his cause for the unification of Italy. He asked Dwight not to publish them immediately.[22] He gave his consent only around 1859.

In these pages he simply noted: "Antonio decided to establish a candle factory and asked me to help him in his establishment. I worked for a few months with Meucci, who didn't treat me like just any other worker, but like one of the family, with a lot of love. So, from sausages he went on to dip wicks." The other patriot, General Giuseppe Avezzana (1797–1879), of merchant ancestry, escaped after the uprisings of 1821 and after a long and profitable stay in Mexico, oversaw sales. He had arrived in New York in 1834 but had returned to Italy during the uprisings of 1849 and had been present in Rome. Since

---

[22] In addition to this version of Garibaldi's *Memoirs there* was another by the Anglo-German writer Baroness Elpis Melena (Esperance von Schwartz), the protagonist of a failed love affair, another by Francesco Carrano and the best known by Alexandre Dumas. All are based on this manuscript drafted by him between 1849 and 1850.

then, he never left Garibaldi. Back in New York he was well received by the Italian immigrants. At the first news of Garibaldi's enterprise in 1860, he hurried to Italy, where he arrived when the hero was already in Caserta, in time, however, to participate in the battle of Volturno.

In 1850, Meucci and Garibaldi went to the Masonic Lodge "Tompkins." It seems that the minutes of the lodge were destroyed in a fire. Garibaldi was initiated into the irregular lodge Asilo de la Verud in Montevideo in Uruguay, and on August 8 of the same year he entered the French lodge Les Amis de la Patrie. It seems that he rarely attended, and when he left for Europe four years later, he was still an apprentice.

Further bad luck: The factory caught fire and was destroyed.

Despite the originality of the kerosene formula, sales were low, and Antonio had to sell all his possessions and change his business by transforming his home into a lager brewery, which was met with much success among villagers, who found in it one of the few satisfactions of life. However, the recklessness or mismanagement of a certain J. Mason, a dealer and swindler, led to the brewery's bankruptcy.

On November 13, 1861, the cottage was sold at auction with everything in it, but fortunately the buyer allowed him to continue living there, even without paying any rent. It was obvious that without a business or employment, the situation continued to get worse and worse.

The situation became more unbearable because of Ester's rheumatoid arthritis, a result of the deadly humid climate of Havana. She eventually was bedridden and remained completely disabled until her death on December 21, 1884.

As they say not all evils bring harm, even if in this case Ester's disability produced unhappiness and serious damage. Pressured by work and the need to always be in contact with her as she lay immobile in bed, Meucci in 1856 installed a small teletrophonic system in the house that connected her bedroom on the third floor with the kitchen and then with the brewery. It was an imperfect system, a magnet and a spool and diaphragm enclosed in a wood and paper box. As he declared to the Circuit Court, he honed the system and commissioned his friend Enrico Bandelari, who was traveling in Europe, to look for competent people interested in the invention who would provide necessary capital for its realization. He then thought of founding a Teletrophone Company but was able to raise a mere $20 of capital.

Chapter 5

The Invention of the Century

The First Electromagnetic Phone

Let's leave aside the many scientists who, throughout the nineteenth century, themselves claimed the invention of the telephone and the whole complex history of attempts to transmit speech. For now, let us remember only that in 1854 Charles Bourseul (1829–1912), around the time of Meucci's first experiments, wrote a memorandum on the transmission of the human voice with electric currents, which he published in the magazine *L'Illustration* in Paris, without, however, having built a prototype.

The one who actually was in competition with Bell was the German Johann Philipp Reis (1834–1874), who was making experiments and prototypes that led to the so-called "Reis's telephone," invented in 1861, the first able to transmit an electrical signal reproducing sounds like the human voice.

However, from secret documents of 1947 preserved in the Science Museum in London it has been revealed that the British industry Standard Telephones and Cables (STC) found that Reis's 1863 type could transmit and "reproduce voice of good quality, but poor efficiency." According to Silvanus Phillips Thompson,

> Professor Graham Bell has not failed to acknowledge his indebtedness to Reis, whose entry "into the field of telephonic research" he explicitly draws attention to by name, in his "Research in Electric Telephony," read before the American Academy of Sciences and Arts, in May 1876, and repeated almost verbatim before the Society of Telegraph Engineers, in November 1877. In the latter, as printed at the time, Professor Bell gave references to the researches of Reis, to the original paper in Dingler's "Polytechnic Journal"...; to the particular pages of Kuhn's volume in Karsten's "Encyclopaedia"..., in which diagrams and descriptions of two forms of Reis's Telephone are given; and where mention is also made of the success with which exclamatory and other articulate intonations of the voice were transmitted by one of these instruments; and to Legat's Report Professor Bell has, moreover, in judicial examination before one of the United States Courts expressly and candidly stated, that whilst the receivers of his own early tone telephones were constructed so as to respond to one musical note only, the receiver of Reis's instrument shown in Legat's Report was adapted to receive tones of any pitch, and not of one tone only. It is further important to note that in Professor Bell's British Patent he does not lay claim to be the inventor, but only the improver of an invention: the exact title of his patent is, "Improvements in Electric Telephony (Transmitting or causing sounds for Telegraphing Messages) and Telephonic Apparatus." (40)

Thompson was expressly concerned in his biography to demonstrate the priority of Reis's invention; he reports the elaboration of the models and the relationships that he puts in synoptic relation with those of Bell, professor of elocution at Boston University and tutor of deaf children, but he ignores the priority of Meucci—he does not even mention him. He mentions Elisha Gray (1835–1901), electrical engineer and co-founder of the Western Electric Manufacturing Company, and the 1876 prototype in Illinois; Cromwell Varley (1828–1883), who in 1870 patented the cimaphene, a kind of telegraph capable of transmitting speech; and Poul la Cour (1846–1908), another competitor in the race between Gray and Bell.

From 1850 the dominant thought and purpose of Meucci's life was the experimentation on this instrument and on the possible means of transmitting the human voice through electrical vibrations. From 1850 to 1871 he developed more than thirty models, with twelve different variations and types of conception. He meticulously kept diagrams, notes, and models of all of them.

The primary objective was to carry out the experiments necessary for the realization of the telephone. The statute provided for the extension of the activities of the company in all European countries with the establishment of subsidiaries, obtaining patents and licenses. This meant nothing, and it would have been risky to present models and projects without applying for a legal patent. The cost to do so was not prohibitive, $250, but still a lot for those times and not doable by Meucci at that time of illness and misery. When the sponsorship of the company's Italian entrepreneurs failed while Meucci tried to find the $250, he applied for a temporary patent at a cost of $15.

Along with the difficulties of using a new language, the isolation of living on an island that was not held in high regard, a port of discharge for ragged immigrants with cardboard sacks and suitcases and garbage from the city, was not propitious. So, in 1852 he contacted manufacturers of Morse telegraph equipment, which was marketed in New York City. He was told that he could purchase the equipment from a "Mr. Chester who lived on Centre Street. In 1854 I obtained reels and other tools from Mr. Chester [and] he showed me all the necessary things then used in the telegraphic [business]. My memory was opened up to build some new tools.... [A]fter some thought, I built a first tool" (Campanella).

He ended up with an instrument in 1854 that used a magnetized rod and a diaphragm with a hole in it and a metal tongue, which he thought was necessary to produce a voice signal. Meucci used a metallic tongue made of platinum; since then, it is understood that platinum is a slightly ferromagnetic material when it contains a nickel impurity. The sound receiver/transmitter he developed was in essence a reversible variable-reluctance transceiver.

Between 1857 and 1858 he asked New York artist Nestore Corradi to make a drawing from his sketch showing "a man in a seated position holding in his hands two small concave-shaped apparatuses attached to electric wires to be used one by mouth to speak, the other to be placed on the ear to receive sounds of the human voice, thus constituting a talking telegraph" and called it a telephone. Corradi, a miniaturist and draftsman, designed the stamp that was shown as evidence in the trial. He had been aboard the *Crocodile* with Meucci, and he too was a stage designer in the Tacón Opera Company under the directorship of Raffaele Patanelli, who staged Donizetti, Rossini, Bellini, and Verdi.

When the company failed because of a risky investment in a French company, Corradi too came to New York in 1852 and, a Freemason and Republican, gravitated to Garibaldi's group of exiles. Naturalized in 1871, he married Mary Dessaa, widow of the famous music professor Anselmo Berti, a friend of Lorenzo da Ponte. In 1863 Ponte had founded and was president of the first Italian mutual aid society, Unione e Fratellanza. His funeral in 1891 was impressive.

In 1860, when Garibaldi was at the height of his glory after the exploits of the Thousand in Sicily, Meucci wrote an article for publication in *L'Eco d'Italia* in New York City describing his "Speaking Telegraph." In the same year Philip Reis brought out the first prototype of his *telephony* (distance speaker), which was a carved wooden "ear" with a membrane made of a pig's bladder stretched over it. Attached to the bottom of the membrane was a platinum lead that opened and closed a battery circuit as it vibrated. The receiver was a coil of wire wound on a knitting needle sitting atop a violin. The body of the violin amplified the vibration from the changing shape of the needle as it was magnetized and demagnetized.[23]

In the meantime, Meucci wrote to Enrico Bendelari, who was in Naples on business, to request that he find him an Italian investor, as Naples already had a vast telegraph network, and sent him copies of his article in *L'Eco*. Attempts to contact

---

[23] See, Huurdeman (154-156) and Harlow (344–348).

the deputy director of the telegraph system of the Kingdom of the Two Sicilies failed. All the contacts had collapsed with the "liberation" of Naples by Garibaldi and the end of the role of the Bourbons in exile. On November 13, 1861, Meucci's cottage and its contents were sold at auction, although he managed to obtain a stay without paying rent.

In November 1865 a man named Innocenzo Manzetti (March 17, 1826–March 15, 1877) had invented a telephone in Aosta: Manzetti directly transmitted the spoken word through a normal telegraph wire with a simpler device than the one used today for dispatches. The possibility of transmitting through electricity vibrations produced by sound was demonstrated with this invention. The news had reached Meucci via *L'Eco d'Italia* of August 19, 1865,[24] and he sent a reply to his Genoese friend Ignazio Corbellino, director of *Il Commercio di Genova*, saying: "I cannot deny Mr. Manzetti his invention, but only want to observe that there may be two thoughts that have the same discovery, and that by combining the two ideas could [one] more easily arrive at the certainty of something so important" (Caniggia Mauro and Luca Poggianti 68).

The newspaper stated on October 21, 1865, that "It now appears that our friend Mr. A. Meucci of Staten Island ... had made a similar discovery, and long before Mr. Manzetti's of Aosta was published in the newspapers. In justice to Mr. Meucci, we publish the following letters that clearly prove that he is at least the first discoverer of the transmission of sounds and spoken voices on a par with telegraphic letters." These were the letters in which Meucci had confided his invention to his friend Enrico Bendelari around 1860.

The first models used the principle of the vibrating ring that Meucci had already experimented with in Havana. Later

---

[24] See Quétànd. Subsequent correspondence occurred through Bendelari.

he replaced the paper cones with tin cylinders to increase resonance. His experiments with thin membranes vibrating by contact with vibrating strips of copper were very similar to today's cup-shaped device.

Between 1858 and 1860 Meucci obtained good results using a horseshoe-shaped permanent magnetic core, a coil, and a diaphragm of animal skin, and in 1864 and 1865 he reached the optimal type. He had replaced the leather diaphragm with one made entirely of metal that could be locked around its circumference thanks to a shaving box whose lid was drilled with holes to obtain an acoustic cone. He called it "the best instrument of my life." It also solved the problems of long-distance communication, which Bell achieved many years later.

Unfortunately, in the extreme poverty that barely allowed him to survive, he could not spread word about his invention. To give us an idea of the means available, let us recall Corradi's drawing, prepared in 1858: a scene illustrating communication at a distance. The racial prejudice of bureaucrats and financiers toward Italians resulted in help only from his fellow countrymen.

In 1861, in the city of great finance, industry, and commerce, Meucci, with his absurd and crazy case, changed tactics and began to look for backers in Italy. A famous Italian opera singer publicized his invention, and that got some feedback in New York's *Echo of Italy*. But there was no response from Italy, which was celebrating the splendor of the first Parliament of the united country.

In 1870 Meucci achieved the transmission of speech at a distance of about one mile. Sadly, on July 30, 1871, he was seriously injured, and his life was left in danger after the explosion of the boiler of the Westfield ferry connecting Staten Island to New York. Meucci remained incapacitated for three months, though he did not give up, even in convalescence working to perfect his project. He and his wife sometimes accepted the charity of alms from friends along with coal, groceries, and a dollar a week from the Supervisor of the Poor of Staten Island until 1880.

It appears that Meucci had already understood well in advance the principle of "pupinization" (which Pupin theorized in 1900), that is, "in the technique of telecommunications, the insertion, at certain and regular distances, of inductance coils (called Pupin coils), on the circuits of a telephone cable in order to reduce the attenuation and distortion of the transmitted signals."[25] Without them, telephone lines cannot reach useful distances.

---

[25] *Enciclopedia Treccani*, s.v., Pupin Michele Idvorsky (1858-1935); he was a physicist and electrician and professor of electromechanics (1901-31) at Columbia University.

The Caveat and Patent Issue

> The great enemy of the truth is very often not the lie—deliberate, contrived, and dishonest—but the myth—persistent, persuasive and unrealistic.
>
> J. F. Kennedy, Commencement Address
> June 11, 1962, Yale University.

Today it seems beyond old-fashioned to talk about the traditional telephone with cable, even though the streets of Italian cities are still being turned upside down for the placement of a new medium, fiberoptics. The cell phone has now become the simplest means of communication, and it also has functions that have very little to do with talking to people, including the phone camera and so on.

Yet this existential revolution is due to the brilliant intuition of Meucci and many others of his time. His idea and its experiments, however, ignited a debate and initiated legal proceedings that resulted in a false attribution and a story of legality invented by modern societies that intend to defend property and commercialize and commodify ingenuity. Patents, as well as copyrights, are the defense of low economic and financial interests. We see in the issue of COVID antiviruses the initiation of disputes and opposing transactions, featuring on the one hand the liberalization decreed by President Joe Biden and on the other the doubts, almost denials, of the EU. In this case we are dealing with a patent that affects the existence of humanity, because if we are not all protected, no one is protected.

The history of telecommunication began with money troubles and courts, because Meucci was dirt poor. This did not happen with the other great Italian, Guglielmo Marconi, and with the telegraph and future communication implications, up to today's TV and satellite transmissions.

Did Meucci in 1862 have a property right or did Bell, who had the money to buy an official patent declaration in 1876? Already in a note of 1857, Meucci had described the apparatus on which he was working: "It consists of a vibrating diaphragm and a magnet electrified by a coiled wire wrapping around it. By vibrating, the diaphragm alters the current in the magnet. These current alterations, transmitted to the other end of the wire, impart similar vibrations to the receiving diaphragm and reproduce speech." If there had been many misfortunes and bankruptcies, in 1861 Meucci was reduced to abject poverty also by lawsuits brought against him by dishonest collectors. He reached the point of having to mortgage his house in Staten Island. Luckily the buyer allowed him to continue living in the house for free. Meucci and his wife managed to survive thanks to welfare benefits and the help of friends.

Fate seemed to be raging against him. During the crossing from Manhattan to Staten Island in July 1871, Meucci was seriously burned by the explosion of the steam engine of the Westfield ferry. When he was left hospitalized for several months, Ester was forced to sell the rudimentary original models of the telettrofono to a junk dealer, Mr. Fleming of Clifton, for six dollars ($6.00).

In the same year, during his convalescence from this accident, Meucci was able to found (together with Angelo Zilio Grandi, Secretary of the Italian Consulate in New York; the entrepreneur Angelo Antonio Tremeschin; and businessman Sereno G. P. Breguglia Tremeschin) the Telettrofono Company, registered on December 12, 1871, in New York, and notarized by Angelo Bertolino. A similar agreement followed in February 1875 with Alexander Graham Bell, Thomas Sanders, and Gardiner Hubbard. The U.S. Patent Office had a caveat, a simple announcement without drawings with intent to patent with a fee of ten dollars ($10).

On December 28, 1871, Meucci filed with the U.S. Patent Office *caveat* No. 3335, *Sound Telegraph*, with a bare description of his invention.[26] Only later did he realize that, to save money, the lawyer had drafted in a half-hour an imperfect specification of the patent, leaving out the most important information. He asked him by letter to correct the inaccuracies, but the lawyer disregarded his suggestions, assuring him that this limited description protected him sufficiently. Perhaps this very superficiality of the description of the invention would have better protected him from copying. The real disaster, as in almost all the initiatives he undertook, was the dissolution of the Telettrophone Company after less than a year, because two of the partners had left New York and withdrawn their shares, while a third partner had died the following year.

In the summer of 1872, Meucci together with his friend Angelo Bertolino introduced himself to Edward B. Grant, Vice President of the American District Telegraph Co. of New York, whose consultants were Alexander Graham Bell and Elisha Gray, and asked for their willingness to test his telettrofono in the telegraph lines of their company. Meucci informed him of his financial difficulties due to the injuries he had sustained in the previous July 1871, his bedridden status, and the sale of most of his instruments by his wife for medical expenses and daily needs.

From 1871 Bell had been working at Boston University, where he taught vocal psychology and diction on an apparatus capable of transmitting musical notes and words. Bell

---

[26] *Caveat*, a subjunctive of the Latin *caveo*, "beware," was in U.S. patent law a warning, in effect a "reservation" or "pre-emption" formula for a patent with a description without details of the invention, pending submission of the actual application. It expired after one year, was renewable and included a fee. As appears in the famous mosaic of the House of the Tragic Poet in Pompeii (Regio VI, Insula 8, n. 5), among the Romans the verb was popular and was inscribed at the entrance, *cave canem*, "beware of the dog."

was born in Edinburgh and moved with his family to Brentford, Canada. Together with his father, grandfather, and brother, he had devoted himself to the question of language and elocution, having as something of an obsession a universal mission of compensating for deafness, from which his mother and then wife suffered.

Grant promised Meucci that he would contact him soon for a demonstration and, confident in the interest he found, Meucci had the ingenuity to leave him a description of the prototype and a copy of the temporary patent. Grant assured Meucci that he would "put at my disposal the telegraph lines needed, provided I would bring in an exact explanation of the mode of operation of the affair, and some drawings, and also some instruments to speak." Meucci reproduced his teletrophone as best he could with makeshift parts and gave it to Grant who did not seem to recognize the merits of these instruments.[27]

After two years without any response to his nagging requests, and after various extensions and generic pretexts, in 1874 Meucci requested the "restitution of the descriptions" and of the drawings, models, and documents, to which Grant replied that all the material had been lost.

In the meantime, Meucci's poverty reached unbelievable proportions: On December 28, 1874, he failed to borrow the ten dollars ($10) needed to pay the annual fee for maintaining and renewing the caveat, and it lapsed, according to patent law.

Of course, this tale seems incredible, since Meucci in that period was able to patent many other inventions of different types for the sum of 35 dollars each between 1872, 1873, 1875, and 1876. Among these we remember, between 1872–1873 (at the request of the diver William Carroll), the construction of a

---

[27] Meucci testimony, Bell vs. Globe, answer 94.

special telephone that allowed an underwater diver to communicate with his ship. But it was only on July 8, 1880, Meucci forwarded the patent application for this device.

According to affidavits, it was in 1877 that Henry brought "some Bell instruments that were placed in the hands of the American District Telegraph Company for I don't know what purpose to Frank's house for testing on a telegraph line between the brothers' homes." It was said that the instruments "worked well, and they spent two or three hours talking."[28]

Bell confirmed that since 1860 he had observed his father and grandfather in their physiological experiments on speech utterances and vibrations and in the teaching of deaf students to produce sounds with their vocal organs. In addition, he became aware of Helmholtz's works on tone sounds with an electric tuning fork[29] as well as those of Wheatstone, who had reconstructed a speaking machine suggested by Baron von Kempelen. Alexander and his brother Melville attempted to build the same device from artificial vocal cords driven by the wind chest of their parlor organ.

Bell knew nothing about electricity and magnetism before he started teaching in Boston, hence his statement about "my crude telephone of 1874–1876." Only in October 1874 did he announce "his intent to patent a telephone" (Grosvenor and Wesson 69). For his telephone experiments from March to May 1875 he used the Western Union facilities in New York, assisted by Henry Pope and George Prescott. In May 1875 Bell announced the addition of variable resistance to his initial telephone design. On January 30, 1876, he signed the patent for "Improvement in

---

[28] Ref, 1, p 166-168. 12; Ref. 1, p 180.
[29] Hermann von Helmholtz (1821-1894), the chancellor of physics, worked on optics, acoustics, and nerve signal propagation ("Any vibratory movement of air in the ear canal, corresponding to a musical sound, can always, and always in only one way, be regarded as the sum of a number of vibratory movements, corresponding to the partial sounds of the sound considered").

Telegraphy," to which was added, "The method of, and apparatus for, transmitting vocal or other sounds telegraphically, as herein described, by causing electrical undulations, similar in form to the vibrations of the air accompanying the said vocal or other sound, substantially as set forth" (Bell 1876, 4).

On February 14, 1876, two caveats were presented within two hours. Mr. H. H. Patrik and Gardiner Hubbard's attorneys filed a patent application on behalf of Prof. Alexander Graham Bell (1847–1922), employed at Western Union Laboratories, for his device to safeguard the "method and apparatus for transmitting the voice or other sounds telegraphically ... by means of electrical waves, similar in form to those accompanying the emission of the voice and sounds in the air." The other caveat was presented unbeknownst to Bell by Mr. Jonathan on behalf of Elisha Gray of Chicago who worked on a simple "telephone with a liquid microphone." In 1877 he founded the Bell Telephone Company, the world's first telephone company.

On March 7, 1876, Bell was issued Patent 174,465 for his "Improvement in Telegraphy," "aimed at performing multiple message telegraphy." Here an armature moving near the pole of a small electromagnet produced an undulating current. Bell also cited "another mode ... where motion to the armature (is) by the human voice or musical instrument" and a "corresponding claim."

On March 10, 1876, Bell demonstrated the conversion of words into electrical current, using variable liquid resistance documented in a second patent. His assistant, in an adjoining room in Boston, heard Bell say the famous words into his experimental telephone, "Mr. Watson, come here, I want to see you" (Bell 1876).

As soon as Meucci learned of the patent, he claimed priority for the invention. According to the dates it was technically ascertained: He had submitted the caveat in 1871 and had renewed it for three years until December 28, 1874. Bell would later declare under oath that he had had his first idea for the electromagnetic telephone in the summer of 1874. Years later, Meucci's precedence would be based on the fact that Bell's patent did not constitute "new and useful art ... not before known or used in this country, and not patented or described in any whichever printed publication, in this or other countries, and that has not been publicly used or sold for more than two years from the date in question." He protested tenaciously, but to no avail, and claimed paternity of the invention, sending numerous letters to newspapers, but his application prior to both had now lapsed.

On June 25, 1876, Bell introduced his telephone in Philadelphia at the Centennial Exposition. On March 13, 1879, New England Telephone and Bell Telephone merged into the National Bell Telephone Co., and on April 17, 1880, National Bell agreed with Western Union to become the American Bell Telephone Company. Finally, in March 1885, American Telephone and Telegraph (AT&T) was merged into Bell Telephone "as a subsidiary of Bell Telephone to build and operate a long-distance telephone network."

In the meantime, Meucci, following inefficiencies in the Bell Company after 1880, established in 1883 a syndicate, the Globe Telephone Company, "for the purpose of carrying on some part of its business out of the State of New York ... and the names of the town and county in which the principal part of the business of said Company within this State is to be transacted are the City and County of New York." Globe, using Meucci's inventions, planned to build and sell telephones, as well as wires, switchboards, and insulators, at competitive prices. Meucci would enjoy a salary of $150 per month until 1886.

As with the New-York District Telegraph Company, in 1872 unsuccessful attempts were made with the Telephone Company and the Globe Telephone Company in Philadelphia.

Although it was rumored that Meucci had earned one hundred thousand dollars, he described the reality to his brother, saying: "I do not like to give bad news: so, I just write to no one; you know and all know well how much I have worked and how much I still work, but now I have only to work the road that leads to eternity. ... All lost and I live for alms, this is what I can tell you and no more not to sadden you. I would like to be there to rest my bones" (Respighi 23).

However, the evidence gathered by Globe gave hope that the High Court would accept the truthfulness of the statements in the complaint it filed at the end of 1885 with the U.S. Department of Justice, where Bell's patents were challenged as invalid based on Meucci's caveat of five years earlier.

It was at the trial that Meucci, by now seventy-seven years old, was able to give his detailed deposition with the chronology of his research and the exhibition in support of all his previous models in an accurate memorandum.

Ten years had passed since 1876 when Bell had filed his patent. In March 1886, the trial began in the case of The American Government vs. Alexander Graham Bell and the Bell Company, with the accusation of fraud, collusion, and deception to obtain the patent. The trial lasted for eleven years, ending in 1897 with the death of the judge and also because Bell's patent had expired. Something should be said about the delays in the judicial system or perhaps the failure of law when a plaintiff must be at the limit of misery just to get satisfaction. As if to say that to get it you have time to die.

While the U.S. Federal Court was dealing with Meucci's lawsuit, which was supported by many affidavits from citizens of Staten Island and New York attesting to his research and achievements, just two days after the start of the trial, the U.S. Government's lawsuit against Antonio Meucci began, with Bell suing Globe for patent infringement in the Southern District Court of New York, presided over by Judge William James Wallace. It was clear that this could resolve the first trial, as a similar case cannot be tried twice. This one took place in a difficult climate of translations of Meucci's deposition into Italian, often misunderstood and disputed by the witness Charles R. Cross, an engineer at the Massachusetts Institute of Technology.

Meucci, moreover, would have had to demonstrate that his invention was prior that of Bell. In 1872 he had given to Edward B. Grant a description of his prototype and a copy of his caveat. When two years later he asked for his documents back, Grant apparently told him they had been lost. He could have established a *terminus antequam* to the invention in the article from the *Eco d'Italia,* where it was described, but it was discovered that that edition had been burned in a fire. It was not possible to find any copies of the articles that had mentioned Meucci's telephone, although the Globe had offered one hundred dollars for all issues from 1859 to 1862. By 1885 the entire collection of *Eco d'Italia* owned by Dr. John Citarotto had been sold to the Bell Company for $125. The editorial collection was missing many issues from 1857 to 1881 and 1859 to 1863. Nevertheless, many details appeared in Meucci's thorough deposition, collected in the 214 pages with descriptions of the thirty devices created from 1849 to 1865.

At that time Meucci presented as one of the most important proofs his diary, published by Rider & Clark, in which drawings and notes from 1862 to 1882 were reported. Upon presenting this he was accused of producing these notes after Bell's invention and backdating them. Against the prosecuting attorney's evidence that Rider & Clark had only been founded in 1863, Meucci countered that one of the founding editors, William E. Rider, had personally given him a copy of the journal as early as 1862. It is said that the judge, prototypical of the Trump opponents of immigration, did not believe him. But it was and is law that a mere personal word cannot be considered evidence without the concrete object.

The turning point for the declaration of non-prosecution occurred on July 19, 1887, when Judge William Wallace in the case *The United States v. Antonio Meucci* issued his ruling in favor of Bell. According to Wallace, Meucci was unable to present sufficient elements, either in the temporary patent or elsewhere, that contained elements of an electric telephone that would constitute precedent over Bell's patent. He also refuted Meucci's claim that he knew the key principles of the invention; Meucci's device would have been an elaborate corded telephone. Therefore, consequential to the terms of the complaint was the conviction of malice in attempting to defraud investors. Wallace decided in favor of Bell, accepting Cross's opinion that "they were little more than a toy string telephone."

The sentence stated: "There is no evidence that Meucci obtained any practical results other than conveying speech mechanically through a cable. He undoubtedly employed a mechanical conductor and assumed that by electrifying the apparatus he would have obtained better results." Historian Giovanni Schiavo considered the sentence as "one of the most glaring miscarriages of justice in the annals of American justice" and "one of the most dishonest sentences in the annals of America and not only dishonest, but outrageously offensive" (Schiavo 102).

There were therefore neither winners nor losers in this marathon of lawyers who certainly profited from Bell, who was already exploiting the invention. But whereas Bell received the earnings from the patent, Meucci between 1878–

1880 was reduced to such a degree of misery that the supervisor of the poor of Staten Island gave him a small cash grant.

His was a life dedicated to discovery, so when during the interrogation he was asked: "What business did you undertake after you gave up the candle factory?" his answer was "Nothing; as I have done with all my life-experiments."

Meucci did not give up and continued the judicial struggle: In March 1886, he filed a complaint in southern Ohio, which was dismissed January 1886; in January 1887, he filed a Bill of Complaints in Massachusetts, but in November 1887 the judge upheld the lawyers' recusal by Bell. The government appealed to the Supreme Court and, dismissing the verdict, reopens the trial.

He still hoped that his claim to priority would be recognized and on June 12, 1889, a few months before his death, he wrote to his friend Montelatici in Florence, "I am shouting about it, but the others have all the cards. In any case, it is up to the Court of Appeals to make the final decision" (Respighi 23).

Finally in 1887 he gave up, after a series of trials lasting twelve years and involving eighteen thousand pages of documents and depositions, never published but available today. He had devoted his life to a project, in between complaints about Bell and petitions to the government. Yet, Bell's 1876 patent would expire in 1893 and everything would become "moot." But there was some measure of posthumous satisfaction: On November 1897 the Supreme Court closed the trial for "consent as moot."

Throughout the rest of his life, he would continue to repeat, "I invented it and first made it known, and that, as you know, was stolen from me." Having been sick for some time and many years a widower, he grew worse in October, and, continuing to repeat his ramblings about inventions and telephones, on Friday, October 18, 1889, at 9:40 a.m., alone and in extreme misery,

Meucci died at the age of eighty-one in his Clifton home, shortly before the Globe Telephone Company filed its judgment, though confident that he would obtain full recognition of his invention. Persecuted until his death by the blackest misery, he was given a solemn and grandiose state funeral by the Italian community and many of the Americans who loved him, at the expense of the Italian government in posthumous recognition of his extraordinary gifts. His ashes rest together with those of his wife in the Garibaldi-Meucci Museum of Staten Island, where he lived for almost forty years.

The cottage, already sold to a brewer of the island, was donated by him to the Italian Colony and surrounded by the fence one can see today. His furnishings and personal objects, along with Garibaldi's heirlooms, had a worse fate. In testamentary dispositions he had arranged for a gift of one hundred dollars to each of the two little daughters of his friend Nisini who had assisted and cared for him in the desolation of his last years. The auction of all personal effects and furniture yielded $191, which was not enough to cover expenses. The bed where Garibaldi had slept was sold, as old iron, for seven francs.

Meucci's brother Giuseppe received no compensation or reparation from the Bell Company, which had entrusted the matter to the executors of his will, despite the interest of Hon. Luciani and other high personalities, even the Italian Ministry of Foreign Affairs. Meucci had hoped that at least his family and his dear brother Giovanni would enjoy the fruits of his labor. On August 2, 1880, he wrote: "Hope well: If business is good for me, you will be happy even after my death."

Again, on December 6, 1886, he had hoped, writing, "My business is not yet finished: We hope that it will come to light and end after my death." As late as 1891 Giuseppe wrote to the director of the *Rivista Italo-Americana* for news about the inheritance (Respigjhi 71-72).

The interventions of the American press in favor of the priority of Meucci's invention had a certain resonance but did not achieve practical effects, despite the expansion of Fascism in American public opinion and among many immigrants. Some time had passed since Mussolini had collaborated with *Il Proletario*, organ of the Italian Socialist Federation in Philadelphia, and even entertained some temptation to emigrate to America, as reported by the anarchist Carlo Tresca (director of the newspaper and friend in Switzerland, who was assassinated in New York, January 11, 1943, presumably by the Mafia).

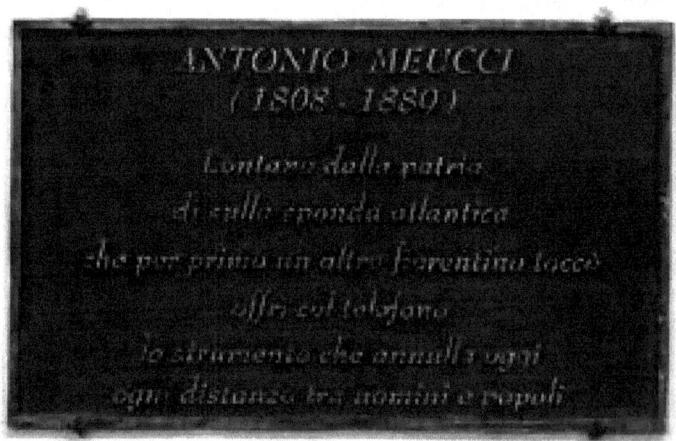

Tombstone of Antonio Meucci

Luigi Barzini, celebrated editor, and correspondent for *Corriere della sera* in New York from 1921 to 1931, wrote a vindication of Meucci's case (Barzini), an article in *Il Corriere d'America*, in the very last year of his ownership.[30] We can remember the

---

[30] The newspaper was founded by Barzini on December 27, 1922, after Carlo Barsotti refused to sell him *Il Progresso italo-americano* (which he directed from 1879 to 1928). He obtained a loan from Pio Crespi, who was living in Dallas at the time, and the newspaper reached a circulation of 50 thousand copies the following year. In 1928, after the failed attempt of purchase by the Order of Sons of Italy, the

interventions of the *New York Times* and the *World* of October 19, 1889, and the statements of A.P. Ulman. Then nothing. Even H. A. Frederich's document of on the development of the telephone published in 1931 in the *Journal of the Acoustical Society of America*, among all the cited precursors of the telephone the name of Meucci is not even mentioned (Frederich).

Resuming the Issue: Half Recognition

After the intense journalistic campaign during the Bell/Globe trial and the numerous obituaries, vulgarly called "crocodiles," at the time of his death on October 18, 1889, both in the international press and in public opinion, silence fell on the injustice done to Meucci, with very few praiseworthy but sporadic exceptions. These included the conference of Italo Brunelli, inspector of telegraphs, in May 1900; or the bust of the sculptor Mancini presented to Minister Pascolato on June 17, 1901, by the Telephone Company; or the photo of Meucci as the inventor of the telephone on the cover of the subscriber list of the Telephone Company of Upper Italy. Therefore, Umberto Bianchi wrote: "The future will repair this guilty neglect, which, moreover, shows how little esteem the Italians themselves still have for themselves and their virtues and things."

It was only in August 1922 that the magazine *Telegrafi e Telefoni* acknowledged the merits of Bell (who died on August 2) and timidly admitted Meucci's important contribution. The following year, in March 1923, there was a great turning point with

---

newspaper was bought by the entrepreneur Generoso Pope, who beat out the competitors of the International Paper Company and thus owned also *Il Progresso*, *Il Bollettino della Sera* of New York, and *L'Opinione* of Philadelphia. This was the great promotion of Fascist propaganda in the US, which also made use of many radio stations and countless other broadsheets, as well as newspapers and periodicals, such as *Il Grido della Stirpe* of the former anarchist Domenico Trombetta and *Il Carroccio* of De Biasi. In San Francisco, Ettore Patrizi, "the little Fuhrer of California," published *L'Italia* and *La Voce del Popolo*.

a question and request for an answer written by Umberto Bianchi, written to Benito Mussolini, asking him to decree an official inquiry into Meucci's priority in the invention of the telephone. The following year saw publication of a text on the results of Meucci's research, and on September 16, 1923, the inauguration of the monument to Antonio Meucci in front of the house in Clifton in the Garibaldi Memorial took place on the initiative of Capt. Cuomo Cerulli and the Italian community.

The real revival of the Meucci issue took place during the well-established Fascist era, in that climate of revenge just before the condemnation of the conquest of Ethiopia by the League of Nations and Mussolini's national-patriotic exaltation on October 2, 1935: "Italians, A People Of Poets Of Artists Of Heroes / Of Saints Of Thinkers Of Scientists / Of Navigators Of Transmigrators," as it still reads in Rome on the four façades of the Palazzo della Civiltà Italiana or the Palazzo della Civiltà del Lavoro at EUR.

The initiator of this re-examination of the Meucci question was the brilliant Guglielmo Marconi, then president of the CNR (National Research Council), who had fully and unreservedly acknowledged his revolutionary invention that would, together with the telephone, open a new era in the history of mankind. In 1930 he published a memorandum on the news available in Italy about Meucci's contribution to the invention of the telephone.

It is not that Marconi had better luck raising capital in Italy, but his mother Annie Jameson's Irish ancestry and his father's economic solidity made it easier for him to found the Wireless Telegraph Trading Signal Company in 1897 and win the Nobel Prize in 1909. From the provisional application of March 5, 1896 (No. 5028, "Improvements in telegraphy and related apparatus"), twenty-one days before the transmission of the Russian Aleksandr Stepanovič Popov (1859–1906), he went on to confirm acceptance on March 19 and the final application

(No. 12039, "Perfections in the transmission of impulses and electrical signals and related apparatus") on June 2, to the patent of July 2, 1897.[31]

It had become the symbol of Fascist Italy, to be exported and proposed even to the decree that "the day April 25th, anniversary of Guglielmo Marconi's birth, is declared, to all effects, a day of civil solemnity in accordance with the law March 28th 1938, n. 276 G.U. N. 84 of April 12th 1938, Vittorio Emanuele III" (repealed 2008).

In 1932, Mussolini's government entrusted Guglielmo Marconi, then president of the CNR, with the task of organizing the Italian participation in the 1933 Chicago Century of Progress Exposition. Between 1931 and 1932, in collaboration with the Museum of Science and Industry of Chicago-Science Hall, an archive of objects and documents of the Italian scientific tradition was created. The Italian Pavilion, designed by architect Adalberto Libera, in the rationalist architectural lines of the time in line with the processes of Science and Technology, expressed the functions of the exhibition.

The government intended to enhance and publicize on this international stage Italy's scientific and technological advances and to celebrate the nation's contributions to communication. It was a delicate moment in the European equilibrium with the rise of Hitler's Germany, and Meucci could best represent Italian genius with the "invention of the century." The project was excellently represented by the Documentary Collection of Italian scientific and technical records, created by Giulio Provenzal,[32] and used to prepare the exhibition, at the request of Mus-

---

[31] Marconi Fund in the Historical Archives of the Accademia Nazionale dei Lincei; Marconi Archives, Bodleian Library in Oxford and Museum of the History of Science; Archives of Institution of Engineering and Technology in London.

[32] *Documentary Collection of Italian Scientific Primates - CNR - Historical Archives - Museoscienza*. From a family of Jewish origin in 1938, with the enactment of the racial laws, he is removed from employment and public life and during the

solini, to demonstrate Italy's contribution to world civilization. It followed the work of Luigi Respighi, Meucci's greatest expert (Respighi 72),[33] who, through the letters of Giorgio Diaz de Santillana (Italian American physicist and historian of science), Ernst Feyerabend, and Paul J. Collura, supported the priority of Meucci's invention. Enrico Fermi in a 1929 letter stated that he did not have enough documents to take a solid position. Also supporting Meucci was the classical philologist Sebastiano Timpanaro (1923–2000) with his essay "Illuminazioni scientifiche. Antonio Meucci e il telefono."

In view of this exhibition, in 1933 Marconi commissioned the Officine Galileo to reconstruct four copies of the two most important versions of the telephones made by Meucci, those built in 1857 and 1867, and to send one of them to Chicago. They are preserved today at the museum of the Rai in Turin, at the former Sirti museum, and at the National Museum of Science in Milan. Photos of copies, earlier models, and a copy of the caveat are exhibited at the Garibaldi-Meucci Museum in Staten Island. These were the result of investigations and a report from the Catanese lawyer Francesco Moncada through original documents traced and collected at that time in New York and reconstructed from original notes and sketches.[34] Unfortunately, Moncada died suddenly as soon as he returned to Italy. On the initiative of Marconi, a couple of the copies were sent to the International Exhibition and are preserved. The two models were the same as those in the 1885 circular of the Globe Telephone

---

German occupation and thus forced to go into hiding.

[33] Respighi's *Per la priorità di Antonio Meucci nell'invenzione del telefono* was published by the Comitato Nazionale per il bicentenario della nascita di Antonio Meucci. It is divided into a collection of documents on the first claims in Italy, the American press, the telephone at the Philadelphia Electricity Exhibition, Meucci and Bell caveats, precursors and priorities, negotiations, and trials, Meucci's autographs. See also Umberto Bianchi.

[34] The Meucci-Catania Archive was donated in 2012 by the heirs to the Marconi Foundation at Villa Grifone.

Company which claimed Meucci's priority in the invention of the telephone. The display at the Italian pavilion, where on the walls was affixed a blow-up of the page of the Chicago *Tribune* listing Meucci's achievements, alarmed Illinois Bell.

In the climate and ambitions of Fascist nationalistic patriotism, it was logical to focus on the unresolved dispute between Antonio Meucci and the giant A.T. Bell over the paternity of the invention of the telephone. It was obvious that there would have been an immense media prominence in that limelight, given the worldwide reality of the need for the telephone and the rivers of money that manipulated the Bell Telephone Company, today's AT&T (American Telephone and Telegraph). The precise historical reconstruction of the facts through new documents provided by Marconi's CNR gave immense echo to the issue, framed among "The Primates of Italian science and technology."

Since then, investigations and studies have become more methodical and thorough. Valuable research has been done by Giovanni Schiavo in 1958 and by Basilio Catania in 1998. The latter found an article that cited a claim by Meucci to have invented a Sound Telegraph before 1870. His research led to the discovery of other documents in Italy in the libraries of Florence and Rome, but also in Havana; Washington, D.C.; Staten Island; and in Bayonne, NJ, and still others in the US National Archives.

In 1994 Catania found evidence in a translation of Meucci's laboratory memorandum by lawyer and acquaintance Michael Lemmi of a test wiring from 1862, consisting of a large coil of wire in the middle of a long transmission line. Such an inductive loading phenomenon was discovered by Michele Pupin (1858–1935) about thirty years later, eighteen years after the 1883 trial, and he obtained a patent for it in 1900.

However, the question of the paternity has always been debated with options and proofs, but it has never reached a legal, certified, and accepted certification. As a more serious offense to the historical truth, still in some schoolbooks and encyclopedias we continue to attribute to Bell the discovery that has given a different course to the history of mankind, up to the complete slavery to that invention today with the Internet and, even more, with cellphones.

The historic stage of the official recognition of Meucci's priority was a speech by Basil Catania at New York University on October 10, 2000, which was advertised as follows: "The vindicator of Meucci's rightful place in the forgotten pages of American history. In 1999 in Havana, the judge of the Supreme Court of the State of New York, Hon. Dominic R. Massaro, had dubbed him "Meucci's Vindicator." And finally, shortly after the approval of the Resolution of the Congress of the United States recognizing Meucci's claim, Catania was officially recognized by the Order of the Sons of Italy in America as the inventor's "Vindicator," with a certificate conferred on October 12, 2002, and with a press release of the following November 21. Catania's NYU lecture gave impetus to the initiative of Peter Vallone, New York Council Member (1986 to 2001), to present to the Council resolution No. 1556, to recognize the priority of Meucci's invention of the telephone, a resolution that passed unanimously (Catania 2004).[35]

Peter Vallone, New York Council Member

---

[35] Catania's lecture was in 2000 at NYU's Casa Italiana and later published in 2004.

Res. No. 1566 Title Resolution calling upon the United States Congress to acknowledge the primacy of Antonio Meucci in the invention of the telephone and declare his moral vindication for this great achievement in the service of science and all mankind. Body By The Speaker (Council Member Vallone) also Council Members Berman, Dear, Malave-Dilan, Henry, Koslowitz, Marshall, Michels, Nelson, Rivera, Robles, Abel and Stabile; also Council Members DiBrienza, Eisland, Fisher, Harrison, Lasher and O'Donovan Whereas, One hundred and fifty years ago, the great Italian inventor Antonio Meucci arrived in New York City and embarked on the defining chapter of a career both extraordinary and tragic; and Whereas, Absorbed in a project that he began in Havana, an invention that he later called a "telettrofono," involving electrical communications, Antonio Meucci immediately began to pursue his aspirations with ceaseless vigor and determination; and Whereas, Mr. Meucci resumed the experiments he began in Havana in his new home in New York, communicating with his wife via a rudimentary electronic line that went from the basement to the first floor; later when his wife began to suffer with crippling arthritis, he put up a permanent line between his lab and his wife's bedroom; and Whereas, Having exhausted most of his life's savings in pursuing his work, Antonio Meucci was unable to construct a model for his invention, though he demonstrated his instrument in 1860 and had a description published in a New York Italian-language newspaper; while he eventually became a proud American citizen, the inventor never learned English, making his path in the American business community more trying; and Whereas, Antonio Meucci was unable to raise funds to pay his way through the long, labyrinthine patent application process and was forced to settle for a caveat, a one-year notice of an impending patent only to learn that the Western Union affiliate laboratory had lost his models and Meucci, who at this point was living on public assistance was forced to allow the caveat to lapse at the end of 1874; and Whereas, In March, 1876, Alexander Graham Bell, who performed experiments in the same laboratory that Meucci used, and where his materials were stored, was granted a patent and was, of course, credited with inventing the telephone;

and Whereas, It should be recalled that if Antonio Meucci could have paid the ten-dollar fee to maintain his caveat, that the Bell patent could not have been granted; and Whereas, In January, 1887, the Government of the United States moved to annul the patent issued to Alexander Graham Bell for fraud and misrepresentation; the case was found meritorious and viable by the United States Supreme Court, which refused to uphold a dismissal, and remanded the case to a lower court; and Whereas, Antonio Meucci died in 1889, and the Bell patent was to expire in 1893, causing the case to be discontinued as moot without a resolution ever being reached as to the underlying issue of who invented the telephone; and Whereas, The Secretary of State of the United States had, at the time of the dispute, stated publicly that "there exists sufficient proof to give priority to Meucci in the invention of the telephone"; and Whereas, The Council of the City of New York has not forgotten Antonio Meucci's great contributions to science and to humankind, and to the end of preserving his legacy, has by proclamation declared May 1, 2000 to be "Antonio Meucci Day"; now, therefore, be it Resolved, That the Council of the City of New York calls upon United States Congress to acknowledge the primacy of Antonio Meucci in the invention of the telephone and declare his moral vindication for this great achievement in the service of science and all mankind.

Following the above-cited resolution, Democrat Congressman Eliot Engel of New York introduced House Resolution 269 to recognize Meucci as the inventor of the telephone. On June 11, 2002, Republican Jo Ann Davis (1950–2007) of Virginia proposed suspending House rules and accepting resolution 269. Hearing other statements from representatives, the resolution was approved by a two-thirds majority. Catania then declared: "This Florentine takes his place among others such as Dante, Michelangelo, Galileo, Lorenzo Ghiberti and Machiavelli." Jo Ann Davis, in turn, stated: "Meucci should be remembered with other innovators, like Edison, the Wright Brothers, and Marconi whose vision and tenacity changed our lives for the better."

Among many options and categorical stances, the New York congressman representing Staten Island, the Italian American Vito Fossella,[36] presented a House proposal that the U.S. Congress approved on June 11, 2002, as Resolution 269:[37]

> [Congressional Bills 107th Congress]
> [From the U.S. Government Printing Office]
> [H. Res. 269 Engrossed in the House (EH)].
> In the House of Representatives, U.S., June 11, 2002.
>
> Whereas Antonio Meucci, the great Italian inventor, had a career that was both extraordinary and tragic;
>
> Whereas, upon immigrating to New York, Meucci continued to work with ceaseless vigor on a project he had begun in Havana, Cuba, an invention he later called the "telephone," involving electronic communications;
>
> Whereas Meucci set up a rudimentary communications link in his Staten Island home that connected the basement with the first floor, and later, when his wife began to suffer from crippling arthritis, he created a permanent link between his lab and his wife's second floor bedroom;
>
> Whereas, having exhausted most of his life's savings in pursuing his work, Meucci was unable to commercialize his invention, though he demonstrated his invention in 1860 and had a description of it published in New York's Italian language newspaper;
>
> Whereas Meucci never learned English well enough to navigate the complex American business community;
>
> Whereas Meucci was unable to raise sufficient funds to pay his way through the patent application process, and thus had to

---

[36] Born in New York on March 9, 1965, a Republican representative in the House from 1997–2009, he was also credited with the legislation that led to the permanent closure of the Fresh Kills landfill.

[37] Congress.gov. H.Res.269: Expressing the sense of the House of Representatives to honor the life and achievements of 19th-Century Italian-American inventor Antonio Meucci, and his work in the invention of the telephone. Sponsor Rep. Fossella Vito, House, Government Reform.

settle for a caveat, a one year renewable notice of an impending patent, which was first filed on December 28, 1871;

Whereas Meucci later learned that the Western Union affiliate laboratory reportedly lost his working models, and Meucci, who at this point was living on public assistance, was unable to renew the caveat after 1874;

Whereas in March 1876, Alexander Graham Bell, who conducted experiments in the same laboratory where Meucci's materials had been stored, was granted a patent and was subsequently credited with inventing the telephone;

Whereas on January 13, 1887, the Government of the United States moved to annul the patent issued to Bell on the grounds of fraud and misrepresentation, a case that the Supreme Court found viable and remanded for trial; Whereas Meucci died in October 1889, the Bell patent expired in January 1893, and the case was discontinued as moot without ever reaching the underlying issue of the true inventor of the telephone entitled to the patent; and

Whereas if Meucci had been able to pay the $10 fee to maintain the caveat after 1874, no patent could have been issued to Bell: Now, therefore, be it

Resolved, That it is the sense of the House of Representatives that the life and achievements of Antonio Meucci should be recognized, and his work in the invention of the telephone should be acknowledged.

Attestation: Clerk

Fossella, celebrating this historic recognition by Congress, which was only ideal and platonic since the companies set up exploited the patents, thanked the young director of the Garibaldi-Meucci Museum in Staten Island, Emily Gear, who had always been on the front line in the recognition and defense of the rights of American minorities and an admirer of Garibaldi whom she called the "Italian Washington." She pointed out that when Meucci invented the electrophone, Alexander Bell was only two years old.

Chicago World's Fair 1933, Italian Pavilion

Media outreach has also found a place in the new tool of cinema: In 1940 the film *Antonio Meucci. Il mago di Clifton*, by director Enrico Guazzoni, starring Luigi Pavese; in 1970 there was the RAI script *Antonio Meucci cittadino toscano contro il monopolio di Bell*; and in 1965, the Italian Post Office dedicated a stamp to Meucci and Marconi.

CHAPTER 6

THE HERO OF THE TWO WORLDS PRECURSOR OF THE UNITED EUROPE

Suppose Europe formed one state.... In such a supposition, no more armies, no more fleets; and the immense capitals, wrested almost invariably from the needs and misery of the people to be lavished in the service of extermination, would be converted instead for the benefit of the people into a colossal development of industry, the improvement of roads, the building of bridges, the digging of canals, the foundation of public establishments, and in the erection of schools that would tower to misery and ignorance so many poor creatures, which in all countries of the world, whatever their degree of civilization, are condemned by the selfishness of calculation and mismanagement of the privileged and powerful classes, the prostitution of soul and matter.... The basis of a European Confederation is naturally drawn by France and England. Let France and England extend their hands frankly, loyally, and Italy, Spain, Portugal, Hungary, Belgium, Switzerland, Greece, and Romelia will also, and as it were instinctively, cling to them. In short, all the divided and oppressed nationalities; the Slavic, Celtic, Germanic, Scandinavian races, including the gigantic Russia, will not want to remain outside of this political regeneration to which the genius of the century is calling them.

Memorandum to the powers of Europe, October 23, 1860, Royal Palace of Caserta

THE "SECOND EXILE"

In his "preface" to his *Memorie autobiografiche,* Garibaldi states the following:

> Stormy life composed of good and evil, as I believe is the case for most people. Consciousness of having always sought the good, for myself and for my fellow men. And if I did evil sometimes, I certainly did it involuntarily. Hater of tyranny and lies, with the profound conviction that they are the main source of evil and corruption of humanity. Republican, therefore, since this is the system of honest people, a normal system, desired by

most, and therefore not imposed by violence and with imposture. Tolerant and not exclusive, not able to impose my republicanism by force; for example, on the English, if they are happy with the government of Queen Victoria. And if they are happy, their government must be considered republican. Republican, but more and more convinced of the necessity of an honest and temporary dictatorship at the head of those nations which, like France, Spain and Italy, are victims of the most pernicious Byzantism. All that I have narrated in my memoirs can serve history. Of the greater part of the facts, I was eyewitness. (Garibaldi 1888, 1)

The epic biography of Giuseppe Garibaldi fills entire libraries,[38] so we will limit ourselves to giving some summary information as a preamble to his American stay in 1850 in Meucci's cottage.

Garibaldi was born in Nice, which at that time was Italian, on July 4, 1807 (he died on June 2, 1882, in La Maddalena), into a family dedicated to coastal trade, and by 1832 he was a captain in the Merchant Marine. He was excited by the doctrines of Giuseppe Mazzini, whom he met in Geneva in 1833, and like him, was a supporter of Italian unification through political and social reforms. He joined Mazzini's movement of Young Italy and, as well, the revolutionary society of Carbonari. Having participated in Mazzini's failed revolt in Piedmont and sentenced to death, he took refuge in Marseille.

From there he began his adventure in Latin America. In 1839, in Brazil, he met Anna Maria Ribeiro da Silva, the heroine Anita, who was of Portuguese and American-Indian origins.

---

[38] For a synthesis, see A. P. Campanella and A. Scirocco.

Anna Maria Ribeiro da Silva

Lover and companion of arms, she became his wife in March 1842 and bore him four children, Menotti (1840), Rosita (1843), Teresita (1845), and Ricciotti (1847). In Uruguay, Garibaldi fought alongside other Italian exiles as a mercenary for the Uruguayans against the dictatorship of Argentine Juan Manuel de Rosas. Enlisting the Italians of Montevideo, he formed the Italian Legion in 1843. Their black flag was the symbol of Italy in mourning, in the center the volcano was the dormant power in their homeland.

It was in Uruguay that he dressed the men of the legion in the red shirts that became the symbol of the Garibaldini. The deadly use of guerrilla warfare,[39] the opposition to both Brazilian and Argentinean imperialism, the resounding victories in 1846 in the battles of Cerro and San Antonio, made Uruguay

---

[39] "On the definitions, from the most benevolent one of 'guerrilla' to the crescendo of 'pirate,' 'smuggler,' 'head of masses, rogue here and there raccooned' always have devaluative intent when not defamatory whatever the reasons and whether they come from Carlo Pisacane" (Ceva 51–60).

independent and free and spread the myth of his heroism to the world. In 1848 he offered himself to the provisional government of Milan and, when Louis Napoleon intervened with Nicolas Oudinot and his Chassepot rifles against the Roman Republic in defense of the Papal State, at Mazzini's invitation, he took command of the defense of Rome. When the city fell on June 30, 1849, he fled, hunted by Austrian, French, Spanish, and Neapolitan troops. In the tragic flight to Venice, Anita, pregnant with their fifth child, died in the marshes of Comacchio (he bitterly mourned "she who was my inseparable companion in the most adventurous circumstances of my life"). He wandered for thirty-seven days, from the mouth of the Po to the Gulf of Sterbino, where he embarked for Liguria. After various vicissitudes, he was taken over by La Marmora, who treated him with respect but as a man "banished" from his land, the Kingdom of Sardinia. He embarked on the steamer *Tripoli* together with Luigi Corelli and Captain Leggero (Giovanni Cogliolo) and landed in Tunis, but there the Bey, "protected" by French diplomatic pressure, rejected him. Having returned to La Maddalena and been the guest of the mayor Antonio Susini, after a month of rest among fraternal people he embarked on the warship *Colombo* for Gibraltar, but even here the English governor rejected him and gave him six days to leave, arousing the indignation of Garibaldi ("a kick in the stomach to the fallen"): "The affection and the justified gratitude that I have always had for that generous nation made me seem all the more rude, futile and unworthy of such a procedure."

Finally he enjoyed the hospitality in Tangier (hoping to be ready for every event) of Giovan Battista Carpeneti, the Sardinian consul, and of the people of the place, a stay that lasted seven months ("a true port against the storm") in the desire to be able to find "a place as a sea captain," which was the privileged profession of his life: "I passed as quiet and happy a life as can be that of an Italian exile far from the sea and from his loved ones and from his homeland. At least twice a week we went hunting, and we hunted abundantly. Then a friend put a gazette [small boat] at my disposal, and we also went fishing, since fish were abundant on those coasts. The kind hospitality I was offered in the house of Mr. Murray, vice-consul of England, sometimes took me away from my solitary and wild habit. Six months therefore passed in that life, which seemed to me so much more fortunate, as the preceding period had been terrible" (Garibaldi 1888, 252–264).

All these periods in the Mediterranean without concrete solutions remain a moment of ambiguity on the part of all the protagonists, as there was no diplomatic reconnaissance to ascertain approval. The only sure thing was Garibaldi's dream of taking to the sea again, even hoping that the Sardinian government would give him a boat. In antithesis this simply aimed to keep him away from Italy, and was there a thought of returning to the Americas where he had fought General Pacheco?

Given his difficult financial situation as an unemployed man, and with the pride of not depending on anyone, he began to discuss with his Genoese friend Francesco Carpanetto the project of inaugurating a merchant service transporting passengers and various cargo between Genoa and New York. With this in mind, they began to raise funds for the construction (in Genoa or America) of a boat to be entrusted to Garibaldi. The hypothesis was the subject of long discussions about the convenience of building "a timber" in the United States (which would be in the vanguard along with shipyards in New York and Baltimore) and about the costs and possible economic advantages. But the solution appeared expensive and distant in time.

Carparetto, shipowner of the *San Giorgio*, planned to reach

Callao in Peru via the United States and Central America. Thus, "while realizing the difficulty of raising funds for the ship to be entrusted to the exile, Carpeneto then planned that the exile would wait for him in New York, accompany him on his tour of the Americas, and finally they would reach together the Callao from the Pacific." Garibaldi's trip to America did have as its objective to reach the *San Giorgio* in Peru, but it projected doing so by other means, via New York and Central America to the Pacific, to embark thence for the Callao (Galeota Capece 654-655). Carparetto was part of the group of friends and supporters of the "trafila ligure," a ship-owning group that had major interests in Peru. It was assumed that the shipowner was the vanguard of a "Ligurian business plan," which envisioned a full expansion of fairs and markets in the Pacific. On this trip he had an important mission: to bring a statue forged in Italy to the cemetery in Lima.

From Tangier on June 22, 1850, on a U.S. sailing "package," Garibaldi reached Liverpool and on June 27 left for New York, where he would arrive on July 30 after a stormy crossing.

IN NEW YORK FOR "BUYING WOOD"

"Those years of exile were a sad period in his life, a period of fundamental change in his view of the problems of the dreamed of unification of Italy. In 1854, on his return to Italy, he was no longer a Mazzinian as he had been when he left in 1849, but a supporter of the idea of confidently placing in the hands of King Victor Emmanuel II of Piedmont the task of uniting all Italians in an indissoluble state" (Cowie, 61).

The reason for the trip is explained by Garibaldi himself in his memoirs. It had been the idea of Francesco Carparetto, to whom he owed favors and kindnesses, to collect among their acquaintances "a sum sufficient to build a ship destined to be commanded by me to earn my life." It was the mirage of that overwhelming exodus, which had involved all of poor Italy without a future, that horizon that opened up even with so much anguish and nostalgia, interpreted by the popular song "Partono 'e bastimente / pe' terre assaje luntane."[40] He justified himself, but there was certainly regret for being hindered in his greatest and most concrete ideals and not being able to fulfill his political mission: "This project smiled at me. Not being able to do anything for the fulfillment of my political mission, I would have at least occupied myself, working mercantile, to acquire an independent existence, and no longer be dependent on the generous man who had hosted me. I immediately accepted the project of my friend Francesco, and I disposed to leave for the United States where the purchase of the wood had to be carried out."[41]

Was it a realistic and cost-effective proposition regarding the costs and benefits to build "a timber" in the United States, even if the New York and Baltimore yards were state-of-the-art? Cost aside, it would have taken time to raise the funds. Carparetto, owner of the *San Giorgio*, intended to change course to Callao, Peru, via the United States and Central America. He planned that the ship owner would wait for him in New York, accompany him on his tour of the Americas and finally reach Callao together from the Pacific. Everything, however, seems nebulous and uncertain.

Yet, Garibaldi writes in his *Diary*: "I immediately accepted the project of my friend Francesco, and I arranged to leave for the United States where the purchase of the wood was to take place. Around June 1850 I embarked for Gibraltar, from there

---

[40] Neapolitan song *Santa Lucia lontana* by E.A. Mario, 1919.
[41] See Cowie on Garibaldi's second exile. The research and sources of this Australian, who dedicated a lifetime to Garibaldi in the Archives of Turin, Bergamo, Rome, London and Cambridge, are extremely important.

to Liverpool and from Liverpool to New York. In the crossing for America, I was assailed by rheumatic pains that tormented me during a great part of the journey, and I was finally disembarked like a trunk, not being able to move, at Staten Island, in the port of New York. The pains lasted me a couple of months, which I spent partly in Staten Island and partly in the city of New York itself, in the house of my dear and precious friend Michele Pastacaldi, where I enjoyed the amiable company of the illustrious Foresti, one of the martyrs of the Spielberg" (Garibaldi 1888, 264).

To his fellow prisoner and friend Eleuterio Felice Foresti (1789-1858) Silvio Pellico wrote in a letter sent from Rome on April 2, 1852: "You are bound to me by sacred memories of a long misfortune and more by the esteem that you inspired in me at the time and that I still have for you. This is based not only on the knowledge that I have of your intellectual qualities, but on the testimonies that are given to me by many of the constant example that you give of your wisdom and goodness. You are one of those who, besides your generous nature, add the merit of seeing things sensibly" (Garibaldi 264).[42] Accepted in 1835 in exchange for imprisonment the perpetual ban, on October 16, 1836, after fifteen years spent in Spielberg, Foresti landed with the vessel *Ussaro* in New York. In 1838, when Da Ponte died, he succeeded him in the chair of Italian literature at Columbia University. To support civic education he founded the Society of Italian Benevolence. Naturalized in 1841 as E. Felix Foresti, he presided over the central congregation of Giovine Italia for North America. In 1850 he founded the magazine *L'Esule Italiano*. In 1856 he returned to Genoa, where he died.

Carparetto's project could not be realized for lack of

---

[42] The recurrent, acute pains in the joints of the hips, knees and back, caused him a form of paralysis in the lower limbs that made it impossible to move independently.

contributors. They had managed to collect just thirty thousand liras, a sum barely sufficient for a cabotage boat: "but as I was not an American citizen, I would have been obliged to take a captain from that nation, and it was not convenient."

THE UNFORTUNATE LANDING IN NEW YORK

So many things can happen because of an overly imaginative idea. Or too big, ambitious, and economically unfeasible, to buy a ship. And Francesco Carparetto was a man with grandiose projects, in which recklessness and hazard were sometimes doomed to success. His adventurous and reckless life would have still involved Garibaldi in a few years. For the moment the dream was shattered in front of the parsimony of probable financiers who did not glimpse secure earnings.

By now Garibaldi, with his heart full of the promise of becoming the owner, master-commander of a ship, even with the terrible pains that tortured him, was approaching New York. It was the *New York Tribune* that gave the explosive news of his arrival at 10 a.m. on July 30, 1850, after thirty-three days of sailing: "This morning the ship *Waterloo* arrived from Liverpool with Garibaldi on board, the man of world renown, the hero of Montevideo and defender of Rome." And it was news that could not go unnoticed, but make the many, many Italian exiles, patriots, refugees from the Carbonari uprisings of 1821 and 1831 go crazy. Such was the enthusiasm for the arrival of the mythical symbol and legend on the part of the many patriots living there that they posted signs praising the "gallant champion of liberty."

The strong community of Italian exiles, but also the German, French, Hungarian, and Polish patriots, known in the city as "red republicans," were taken by enthusiasm. The arrival was greeted by the waving of the American flag next to the tricolor. Garibaldi, however, already forty-three years old, was almost paralyzed by arthritis and refused any contact. He was accompanied by Major Paolo Bovi Campeggi (Bologna 1814–1874), after the Roman campaign of 1849, where he had lost his right hand, a faithful refugee with him in Africa and then in New York, then with the Hunters of the Alps in 1859 and the Thousand.

Garibaldi in that desperate physical condition landed in the port of Staten Island and had his first stunning encounter with New York at the Staten Island Quarantine Station (twelve buildings), in Castleton, before it was burned down by a mob outraged by the dangers of the presence of a very large quarantine hospital, on the night of September 1, 1858 (Staten Island Quarantine War).[43] Opened in 1799, during a yellow fever epidemic, by 1858 it housed 1,500 infectious disease sufferers as a lazaret. The island was a real ghetto of perdition and pain and moreover a huge garbage dump of the metropolis.

The New York City Landmarks Preservation Commission noted: "lonely and impoverished."[44] He first stayed at the Pavillion Hotel in St. George, Staten Island, where he welcomed only very few visitors. Here he was assisted by the surgeon Valentine Mott (1822–1854), son and assistant of the most famous and great surgeon founder of the New York University School of Medicine, who for health reasons then came to Palermo, Sicily, where he was the first to use chloroform and ether in surgical operations and therefore gained great esteem. He took part in the Sicilian uprisings and was surgeon general

---

[43] *Italian crestomazia: a collection of selected pieces in Italian prose*, New York, NY: D. Appleton & Co., 1846.
[44] The new decentralized facility at Seguine Point was also burned at the beginning of construction. The judge acquitted the arsonists as the lazaretto was a danger to the community, they said because it had neighboring properties. By 1859, two hospitals were created on floating islands. In 1873, a quarantine hospital was established at Rosebank on Bay Street and in 1921 and expanded in 1935, it became United States Public Health Service Quarantine Station. It was not evacuated until 1971.

of the insurgents, but also active in the field as a colonel of cavalry. At the head of 900 men, he escaped the preponderant forces and reached Palermo. He opposed the capitulation of the city and escaped on an English ship. Returned to America, he was professor of surgery at the Medical College of Baltimore, where he founded a public clinic. In California he read the news of new insurrections in Italy but died in New Orleans of yellow fever (Echols and Arbittier).

It was Felix Foresti, a companion in the adventure of the Roman Republic, who assembled a committee for the celebration with all the Italian refugees in New York and set the party for August 10 at the Astor House. Meucci had teamed up with several prominent exiles and distinguished Italians in New York, who had joined the committee to welcome the most famous Italian patriot Garibaldi. Garibaldi, however, was forced by the persistence of serious illness to send a letter to cancel his presence at the banquet. William Cullen Bryant, director of the *Evening Post,* commented on the fact that in his high praise of the hero, an exceptional man, he considered him worthy to be included among the portraits of the "great men drawn by Plutarch."

Jessie White Mario (1832–1906) was seen as the "Joan of Arc of the Italian cause" (Palumbo 77), as Mazzini said, and this was how Giuseppe Garibaldi called her in the dedication under his portrait "to my dearest sister, Jessie White Mario, nurse of my wounded in four campaigns 1860, 1866, 1867, 1870": "In America the deportees aroused indignation and pity, where Avezzana, Foresti, and several others honored the Italian name, and more recently Garibaldi." About Garibaldi Foresti wrote in Cuneo in 1852: "Garibaldi is among us since last August, dear to all and highly esteemed even by Americans. Hope of new things in Italy lightens the burden of the common exile. A great whirlwind threatens Europe. Democracy waves its dart with boldness: Let's hope!" The first years of his exile in America were very sad for our hero. Comforted only by the affection of his friends and especially by the fraternal care of Antonio Meucci, he found an honorable job in the manufacture of tallow candles.

The admirers gathered on the pier waiting for the sailing ship to greet their idol but remained discouraged. Garibaldi, prostrated by arthritis at only forty-three years of age, but also by the pain of defeat and the loss of his wife, was not in the mood to meet people and was escorted ashore in great secrecy. Some instead argue that immobilized by arthritis was lowered with the hoist of luggage. It is shown to the Museum among the artifacts a chair that is presented as used to make him rest.

Then, not completely recovered, still sick and suffering, he agreed to move to Manhattan in the house of the merchant Michele Pastacaldi, disappointing his many followers.

Here he found, in addition to Felice Foresti and Meucci, the already mentioned tenor Lorenzo Salvi who was all the rage in New York not only for his fame, bravura, and fabulous earnings, but also for being considered "the darling of the beautiful women of New York." His impresario and friend, the musician and conductor Max Maretzek, who had rented the cottage at Clifton on Staten Island, was happy to offer it to Garibaldi and Meucci who, longing for a quiet place, moved in at the beginning of October 1850. Maretzek had also chosen it for this bucolic purpose: "Then it was that I rushed from the world, secluded myself in Staten Island with an English Grammar, an English Dictionary, and an English friend, who has expatriated himself to become a citizen of this free and 'enlightened Republic,' and made up my mind, with the assistance of these three indispensable necessaries to my task, to attempt its completion" (Maretzek 1855, 112).

Max Maretzek, born in Brno in Moravia on June 28, 1821,

violinist, composer, and impresario, after some of his performances in Germany, then in Paris, where he had contacts with Berlioz and Chopin, and in London in 1844 at Her Majesty's Theatre, had landed in New York in 1848, where he was hired as musical director at Edward Fry's Astor Opera House. The following year he debuted with his Max Maretzek Italian Opera Company, which included many of Fry's artists. His productions between 1848 and 1850 were numerous and continued from 1854 until 1878 with the American premieres of *Rigoletto*, *Trovatore*, and *Traviata*, before becoming a touring company from Philadelphia to Mexico, as well as Cuba.[45]

This is what Maretzek said in his autobiographical work *Sharps and Flats,* on the occasion of an accident during the Castle Garden [106] season of August 17, 1855,[46] where the opera of *Puritani* had been announced with Mme. Steffanone, Salvi, Badjali, and Marini. "About noon on the same day I received a note from Steffanone, informing me of her inability to appear that evening on account of an attack of chills and fever."

Running to the soprano's house, he implored her, promising to apologize to the audience for any breach of duty. Nothing. So it was that he thought of the appeal "to the kindness of Mme. Sontag. The countess was living on Staten Island, in a cottage near the Narrows; it was nearly three o'clock before I arrived at her house, where I found her in conversation with her husband and with Mr. Sontag Ullmann."[47] And it was an

---

[45] His *Max Maretzek Italian Opera Company* or *The Italian Grand Opera Company* or *Academy of Music Opera Company* was the first major opera company in Manhattan and one of the first major companies in the United States, where it performed from 1849 to 1878. In Music in Gotham online, *The New York Scene 1862–75,* two operas are cited, 172 events conducted by him, 559 events managed.
[46] Built in 1839 as an old fortress in Battery Park in Manhattan, renovated in 1847 as an opera house, closed in 1855 and used as a sorting center for immigrants before the founding of Ellis Island, demolished in 1940.
[47] Herriette Sontag, pseudonym of Gertrude Walpurgis of Koblenz, made Countess von Lauenstein by Frederick William III, wife of Carlo Rossi, a Sardinian

amazing encounter in the Narrows. He had not finished exposing the embarrassing situation when the two gentlemen rose up and accused him of impropriety for making such a suggestion.

In the unfortunate situation where he is accused of poor diplomacy and is shown the door, he appealed to his duty to the audience and the other performers, but her husband replied curtly that he would not sing. It was then that Mme. Henrietta Sontag, "who had listened quietly till now, stopped the conversation," cut the conversation short and said, "this is not a question of dignity nor of money — it is to prevent *a disappointment to the public.*" Take an example, you so-called *divas* of the present day! "I will sing," she proceeded, "only, please, Mr. Maretzek, inform Mme. Steffanone for politeness's sake that I will sing her part, if she has no objections. Further, please ask Mr. Salvi, who also lives on Staten Island, a short distance from here, to pass a moment before going to the theatre, and rehearse with me the duo in the third act."

One can imagine Maretzek's joy: "in a moment I was out in the street on my way to Salvi, who was staying in the candle factory of Meucci, now Bachmann's brewery." It was Ester, Mrs. Meucci, who informed him that he could find the tenor Salvi "in the factory, the building next door." The scene in front of him was so surreal that it suggested a mythical, epic image: "On entering there a great surprise, a Homeric spectacle, struck my astonished eyes. There I beheld in front of a large trough, with their arms bare up to the elbows, the perspiration on their brows, kneading hot, melted, and smelling of tallow, Signor

---

diplomat, toured America with Marietta Alboni. About the date, Maretzek himself writes below: "Mme. Sontag after this season went to Mexico under an engage-ment with Mr. Masson, formerly the editor of the *Trait d' Union*, who had rented the Teatro Nacional; her triumphs in both hemispheres were ended by her untimely death on the 17th of June 1854, at the early age of forty-nine years," of cholera.

Lopenzo Salvi, the great tenor, Giuseppe Garibaldi, the great general, and our friend Meucci, the great inventor." One can also imagine the embarrassment of having to deny the handshake: "The illustrious trio greeted me by extending their wet and greasy hands for a cordial shake, which on this occasion I politely declined." So he warned Salvi, "the pet of the New York ladies," to go immediately to Madame Sontag. And she recommended to him, to take first a sponge bath, to don clean linen, and to put some eau de Cologne on his handkerchief" (Maretzek 1890, 9).

Maretzek tells us how the three of them found themselves in that cottage kneading wax: "The house on Staten Island where Garibaldi, Salvi, and Meucci then lived, once belonged to Mr. Townsend, one of the former proprietors of the *Evening Express*. In 1830 I had rented that cottage for my summer residence and, not using it the following winter, I offered it to Garibaldi, who occupied it with Captain Franchi, his *aide de camp*, and a few of his young followers. There they were living, sustaining themselves by fishing and hunting and baking their own bread."

He explained Garibaldi's pride with an anecdote: "Garibaldi would never accept anything from any one and would not touch even any of the many chickens which I had left on the place and used to send or bring the eggs himself to my house in New York" (Maretzek 10-11). This is how the meeting with Meucci — "the true inventor of the telephone" — took place, whom Garibaldi called "Captain Buontempo" and also "my principal" (Garibaldi 1888, 264-64).

Why did Meucci not find accommodation in his own theater, given the name of the La Pergola theater and the high level of professionalism Meucci had acquired in Havana? This concession of the cottage is mentioned, but it is not clear why he was not hired by the Fry's Theater. A serious hole in our information, but believable given the difficulty of finding a business at that stage of immigration to New York despite the hopes and illusions of changing lives in the city of opportunity.

Maretzek reported: "The following summer, when Salvi and Meucci arrived with Marty's Opera Company in New York, they bought the house and grounds from Mr. Townsend and established a candle factory." In other words, Meucci arrived together with his impresario from Havana in New York. From here their lives would separate. Why did their destinies not remain united in the theatrical field, when Marty continued this activity in Richmond and in other American cities?

Maretzek further adds that "The very same house still exists, only it has been transferred from the right to the left of the road by Mr. Bachmann, who bought the land and built his brewery there."

What is even stranger is that the connection to the island would be long-lasting and the impresario musician would die at Pleasant Plains on Staten Island on May 14, 1897.

Chapter 7

Cohabitation

Staten Island was a place of immigration, the first place that immigrants visited in New York Harbor. There were few vacation villas for wealthy New Yorkers. Among the trees overlooking the shoreline was Clifton's cottage, the wooden cottage with two large rooms on the first floor and four on the second floor. Garibaldi was given the room at the extreme northeast corner. It was a living room, study, and bedroom with a bed made of iron with three mattresses, a washstand, and a few other items that had belonged to Maretzek, all given to Garibaldi as a gift. Garibaldi hung on the wall his deer horn that he, like every good Italian (from all regions, not just Naples), held dear and brought in his wanderings to ward off the evil eye. In the living room, on a perch, was the parrot he had taught to shout: "Long live Italy. Out with the foreigner."

It was a relationship of collaboration and mutual aid. Even Garibaldi devoted himself to the preparation of candles. A few trips to the beach with the adoring host for their common Mazzinian religion. Some visits to New York, it is said that the hero went every Friday to Manhattan to play tressette in a club of Italians, perhaps the Club Settefratese of Stamford, Connecticut.

The hero thus remembered and transcribed those days in the exile of his beloved Caprera:

> New York, 1850. When I arrived in New York I was very depressed: the defeat of the Roman Republic, the death of Anita, the exile. I was not well: arthritis immobilized me, and they had to lower me off the ship with a hoist![48]

---

[48] According to Jesse White Mario (1884, 423–424), things were "very sad for our hero the first years of his exile in America. Comforted only by the affection of

I had no desire to participate in the celebrations that so many Italians and Americans wanted to pay tribute to me. Fortunately, I met Antonio Meucci, who invited me to go and live in his small house on Staten Island, which is now the Garibaldi-Meucci Museum. Antonio also had his own problems: he was putting everything into developing his invention, the telephone. He was using it to talk to his wife from one floor of the house to another.

At my request, he set up a sausage factory to provide work for me and other exiles. But I've always been a terrible businessman, and it ended badly. Meucci closed it down and opened a candle factory, whose land was purchased with the help of the famous tenor Lorenzo Salvi.[49]

Unfortunately, my sailor's hands were not capable of inserting the wick into the candle, so I preferred to do heavy work, causing a stir among my companions: according to them, and according to Meucci, I was not obliged to work. But I hated being paid for doing nothing.

So sometimes I would go to the port, and on the docks, I would offer myself as a sailor — I, who had commanded the Uruguayan fleet! Luckily, a friend from Liguria offered me the command of a ship that would sail from Peru to China.

But that's another story.

And he noted, on the side, above a color portrait of them: "Here on Caprera you can see the candles that Meucci sent me in 1861 to celebrate the Unification of Italy. Below, a portrait of me with Antonio Meucci."[50]

During the hours of relaxation, he would go fishing with Meucci in one of their boats, painted with the three colors of

---

friends and especially by the fraternal care of Antonio Meucci, he found an honored job in the latter's manufacture of tallow candles."

[49] According to Lawrence Vera Brodsky, "Salvi had acquired the candle factory from the exiled Italian hero Giuseppe Garibaldi (1807–1882), who had operated it in 1850–51, when he was 'living quietly' on Staten Island" (338, n53). Maretzek (1890, 10) reports that Garibaldi was Salvi's partner in the enterprise in 1853, but, according to the *Tribune* (February 10, 1851), the hero had left for Nicaragua in 1851 (en route to Peru)."

[50] Located at Sistema Museale di Caprera, Musei Garibaldini di Caprera.

the Italian flag and with a dedication on the side to Ugo Bassi, the patriot who had fought with him in Rome and in August 1849 had been shot by the Austrians in Bologna.

There was no shortage of hunting trips, his favorite hobby, with his rifle on his shoulder and a piece of bread and cheese in his pocket through the forests of Dongan Hills and in the meadows of Great Kills alone in search of game. He didn't know that there were closed periods for hunting and was caught by the police, who believed his good faith.

Here in his room on November 11, 1850, he began to write his logbook (Gnola 40). After the tragic days of the embarkation in Cesenatico and the loss of his wife, it was time to reschedule his life, to "get back in touch" with his profession as a sailor. Hence the return to his youth, when the nautical license had allowed him to enroll in 1821 in Nice in the "Registry of Hubs." Therefore, he embarked on various ships and in 1832 received his second-class captain's license, with a qualification for "gran cabotage."

To recover this nautical experience from November 11, 1850, to February 11, 1854, Davide Gnola, director of the Maritime Museum of Cesenatico has reproduced in full the diary and the documents. The completed analysis can be found in the *Quaderno di appunti nautici* (Notebook of Nautical Notes), kept at the Central Museum of the Risorgimento in Rome, including words of seafaring usage, names of crew members, and lists of things to buy, from candles to chronometers to rat-killing cats with the clarification "I am a son of the people" (Garibaldi 1888, 265). This is Garibaldi's version in his memoirs:

> Finally, something had to be done. A good friend of mine, Antonio Meucci from Florence, decides to establish a candle factory and invites me to help him in his factory. No sooner said than done. I could not get involved in the speculation for lack of funds, since the thirty thousand liras mentioned above were not enough to buy the timber and had remained in Italy; I therefore adapted myself to that work on the condition that I did as much as I could. I worked for a few months with Meucci, who did not treat me like just any other worker, but as one of the family and with great love.

Yet there was something that contrasted with his fighting and active spirit: "One day, however, tired of making candles and driven perhaps by natural restlessness and habit, I left home with the intention of changing jobs. I remembered having been a sailor, I knew a few words of English, and I started on the coast of the island, where I saw some cabotage boats busy loading and unloading goods" (Garibaldi 1888, 265).

You can see the brave, wandering hero fighting in the Mar de la Plata and throughout South America; among sailing ships, guerrilla warfare, and continuous and unpredictable risks, you can see him locked in a basement melting candles, hour after hour, day after day. Meucci too could have invented a more qualifying and original job to earn the little to survive.

Anyone would have been tired. Imagine Garibaldi, who in his forty years had not found a moment's respite around the world. Just look at his wanderings from Europe to Africa after the Roman tragedy. A man with no rest, traveling the world, ever since his father had put him on a ship to trade. Now, when it seemed he had arrived in the vaunted place of the opportunity, of invention, of the explosion of genius, now to survive he found himself making stearine. How had the patent genius come up with such a bizarre and strange product and such an out-of-the-ordinary job?

Therefore, the day came when his dissatisfaction could no longer be contained, although he was grateful to his friend who did not make his hospitality a burden at all. So, the rebellion against that obligatory inertia and the *coup de grâce* took this form: Secretly and without telling his beloved host he went to the port of the island, which was then the port of New York; he says of himself that he was mindful "of having been a sailor." It is not clear what use it would have been to him to know a few words of English as a simple sailor.

The scene is grotesque and painful: to see in a small port of fishermen and cargo boats a man who had been a commander of ships and soldiers in South America and who had fought at the head of guerrilla groups. And it is even more poignant to imagine the hero approaching a "cabotage boat." "I reached the first one and asked to be embarked as a sailor." Here he is, shouting his offer but no one on the ship turns to him, they aren't even listening to him. After who knows how long, "They just listened to me, those I saw on the ship, and went on with their work." Such was the offence, the insult, perhaps the indifference to that man who goes begging for a job. Garibaldi, with his poncho and red shirt, did not give up. Perhaps some other man in that large and busy port would hear him or listen to him: "I did the same when I approached a second ship, and I got the same answer. That is, none, as it had happened for the first one." And he goes on to propose any kind of embarkation port: "Finally I went to another one, where they were working to unload, and asked if I could help with the work." It was humiliating for him, a great ship's captain, who, in order to work, was content to be a longshoreman. In Palermo the porter was called "vastasu" (from the Latin *bastasius* or from the Greek, *bastazo*, "to carry"), and the name in popular language had taken on the meaning of "rough" and therefore "uneducated." And still for this humble task, "I had in reply that they did not need it." Even this refusal does not deter him. He wants at all costs to occupy himself with something, anything, and therefore in the most ruthless humiliation, mortification, and in the annulment of self-love and pride. He prayed, "'But I ask you no mercies,' I insisted": nothing. Not even an answer. And his voice, his prayer almost begged for mercy. "'I want to work to shake the cold' (there really was snow): even less. I was mortified."

It was natural that in this extreme situation the times of success and glory came back to him, to aggravate and make unbearable his present despair. No one needed a commander, but neither did they need a sailor, a longshoreman, a simple cabin boy; no one wanted him. Therefore, no one can imagine his anguish, because no one has been the protagonist of an exceptional life, like his previous one: "I thought back to those times when I had the honor of commanding the Montevideo squadron, as well as the warlike and immortal army. What was the point of all this? They didn't want me!" It had to be an act of extreme courage and confidence in himself and in his abilities that were neither damaged nor questioned by this complete absence of consideration: "I finally repented of the mortification and returned to the work of tallow. Luckily, I had not revealed my resolution to the excellent Meucci, and therefore, concentrating on myself, the spite was less" (Garibaldi 1888, 265). What a miserable consolation!

The sailing years, during the passage to Constantinople with the ship *Cortese* in 1827, when he was robbed by pirates and remained there until 1832, being prevented by the Turkish-Russian war in the Genoese district of Galata from teaching Italian, French, and mathematics—all this was a bitter memory. In February he obtained the license of captain second class with the ship *Clorinda* in the Black Sea, withstood another assault by pirates, and sustained a wound to the hand. In 1833 he returned and met with professor of rhetoric Emile Barrault and thirteen followers of Saint-Simon who maintained the idea that "the man, who, becoming cosmopolitan, adopts humanity for his homeland and goes to offer his sword and blood to every people fighting against tyranny is more than a soldier: he is a hero," as Alexandre Dumas reported (Dumas 17)).[51] Between the Black Sea and the discovery of Mazzini came a radical change of life: "Of course Columbus did not feel as much satisfaction in the discovery of America as I felt when I found someone to take care of my country's redemption" (Garibaldi 1888, 14).

However, a certain embarrassment must have lingered in his heart because of this blatant betrayal, aggravated by the fact that everything had remained hidden, without advice or justification between him and his host. Therefore, after the fact, he tried in his diary to give a reason, to minimize his gesture, and make public amends for his "untimely resolution": "I must confess that the conduct of my good principal toward me did not induce me to my untimely resolution; he was generous with his benevolence and friendship, as was Mrs. Ester his wife. My

---

[51] In 1867 Garibaldi, together with Victor Hugo and John Stuart Mill, promoted in Geneva the first Congress of the League for Peace and Freedom.

condition was not, therefore, wretched in Meucci's house, and it was precisely a fit of melancholy that had driven me away from that house. In it I was very free, I could work if I liked, and I naturally preferred useful work to any other occupation, but I could go hunting sometimes, and we often went fishing with the owner himself and with various other friends from Staten Island and New York, who often favored us with their visits. In the house, then, there was no luxury, but nothing was lacking in the main necessities of life, both for lodging and for food" (Garibaldi 1888, 265–266).

But it was this bourgeois life of humble work, of relative well-being, even in full freedom of action, this, shall we say, "normal" life that could not satisfy a restless soul, always burning to do something. The confession seems to be a surrender to the evidence, but as soon as the time comes, he will take whatever opportunity fate and friends offer him.

For now, in this hermitage he was left with nothing but memories, the nostalgia of a life that was reckless but full of affection. In this abandonment he felt the need to "mention Major Bovi, who lost a limb the defense of Rome, who was my brother in arms in various campaigns." This is what spurred him to return "to Tangier in the house of Mr. Carpeneto, where I spent a period of asylum at one time and when I decided to move to America, not able to employ my means of bringing together with me all my comrades." He remembers his remaining comrades Leggiero and Coccelli, when he took Bovi with him, "unable to work because he was missing his right hand." Coccelli was a "young, handsome, and valiant comrade." "He had entered the Legion of Montevideo as a child; having a great propensity for music, he played the trumpet in the superb band of the Legion and the war trumpet in the famous charges with which that valiant corps made the Italian name respected in America. Coccelli followed the Legion in all its campaigns and was part of our 48th expedition to Italy. He took part with honor, as an officer, in the campaigns of Lombardy and Rome and came with me when, as ordered by the Sardinian government in '49, I went to Tangier. When I left Tangier for America, I left Coccelli my rifle and all my hunting equipment. He died still very young, struck down by too much African sun to the head."

One understands how in that Staten Island that was a prison for him, he felt anguish for those places he still dreamed of and for those beloved people with whom he had shared dangers and glories.

We close this phase of his life with a memory that takes us back to the origins of the vicissitudes of an extraordinary sailor — Ulysses's dog waited for his master and died of happiness when he returned. Garibaldi's experience, however, differed: "My hunting dog Castor, I was also obliged to leave him in Tangier with my friend Mr. Murray, and that faithful companion of mine died of pain" (Garibaldi 1888, 265–266).

MEUCCI TELLS OF GARIBALDI

He lived in a small room, lit by two small windows to the north and south. It has not been touched since the General left; it is in the same state as twenty years ago. It contains an iron bed, an iron basin holder, three chairs, a small table, a wooden toilet with a checkers game on it, and a cabinet decorated with simple but graceful straw work in various colors, on which there is a wax skull. Two small mirrors hang from the bare walls: in front of them Garibaldi often tormented his blond beard with scissors. There is no other furniture. But there is a shirt lying on the bed that makes the heart beat faster for every Italian who sees it, the red shirt that Garibaldi wore during the Rome campaign in 1849 and that he left to Mrs. Meucci as a souvenir. It is made of canvas, with green collar and cuffs edged with white, with ordinary glass buttons. It has the national colors and still bears traces of the sweat of the man who was the greatest factor of national independence. To Mr. Meucci the general gave a magnificent small knife, religiously preserved in its velvet case. This dagger adorned his side in Montevideo: the handle and the sheath of bronze metal are finely chiseled, and the handle is artistically formed with a small group representing Mazeppa chased by dogs.

When Garibaldi disembarked in New York he was poor and owned only the suit he wore. Having lived several years before in South America, Meucci had recently come to settle on the Atlantic coast where he met Garibaldi and invited him into his home. Garibaldi accepted the hospitality. And in that modest house, the free life, the friendliness of the Meucci family and the visits of his exiled patriots, poured a little balm on his heart torn by the memory of his beloved Anita and failed campaigns. How many nights must he have kept vigil in that small room, in solitary meditation!

How he must have quivered with indignation on that bed, thinking of the enslaved country, of the vain attempts of '48 and '49, of the retreat from Rome, of Austria, of France, of the blood shed! In Staten Island Garibaldi was serious, melancholic, of few words. Unable to adapt to the idle life led by many exiles, he was tormented by the fever of motion and work. Some mornings he would leave with his rifle over his shoulder and, with a little bread and cheese in his game bag, he would go into the surrounding woods and would not return home until late at night, when he was tired and full of game. One day he came back without having fired his rifle: "But I didn't come empty-handed, dear Mrs. Ester," he said to Mr. Meucci's wife, placing a white animal in her lap: "I found this young hare, shivering from the cold." The young hare was a kitten, the Eve of the feline breed in the Meucci household. He went hunting one day out of season without knowing it, was arrested, and then released because of the intervention of friends. When he returned home, some people complained in his presence about the American laws, but he observed that the Americans make the laws that are convenient to them, without thinking about foreigners; that Italy, having become a nation, would do the same, and that everyone is obliged to respect the laws of the country in which he finds himself. Some other days he embarked on a pretty boat with a Latin sail that Meucci had bought, painted in white, red, and green, and baptized *Ugo Bassi* in memory of the martyred priest. Garibaldi, a born sailor, flew it over the waves like a seagull and spent whole days and peaceful nights fishing. When he didn't go hunting or fishing, Garibaldi, not to be idle, wanted to help Mr. Meucci and worked first in the manufacture of salami and later in the manufacture of candles. One day, while stripping some ox bones, the knife slipped and cut off a piece of his finger, which fell off and merged with the other meat: "Don't look for it," he said, smiling at the bystanders, "it will make Republican salami!" It is untrue that he ever worked in New York as a salaried worker. Meucci's house on Staten Island was visited as a sanctuary by all the Italian exiles who landed in New York. Garibaldi, however, did not pose as a hero or an oracle before anyone, he was good, sweet, an excellent companion, who every time he realized he had two shirts, he gave one to the man who could not change the one he was wearing. He was often visited by Major Bovi, Righini, Oregoni, General Avezzana, Foresti, Pastacaldi, Filopanti, Minelli, Colonel Forbes, Marinelli, and other illustrious and brave men. Among the Americans who were sympathetic to the Italian cause was John Anderson. Whoever would have stenographed the conversations of those patriots and the magnanimous words and audacious projects and lively hopes that Garibaldi expounded would have adorned the history of Italy with some immortal pages.

Sometimes laughing and forgetting the disillusionment of the past and the uncertainties of the future, they spent some happy evenings, sometimes discussing physical and mathematical sciences and the English language, studies to which Garibaldi devoted several hours each day. But most of all, Meucci and the few old people still living here remember with emotion the good heart and generosity of the general. Mrs. Meucci had a good time stocking his closet with linen! The first poor Italian who showed up asking for help took it away. There was no question of money. It disappeared as if by magic as soon as it entered his pocket. Once, a shipowner who had to entrust him with the command of a ship sent him seven hundred dollars. What did Garibaldi do? He immediately sent for the neediest exiles, without wasting a minute laid the sum on the table, made as many piles as there were people present, except for himself, and fraternally distributed them. And at that time, he owned only two shirts: "You see," he said, "man is born without a shirt: I, who own two shirts, can give one as a gift." This is Garibaldi.

Here are some interesting details that Adolfo Rossi (Correspondence from New York to the League of Democracy, August 2, 1882) collected from the mouth of Meucci himself, being a guest of the general at that time (Mario 423–424).

GARIBALDI'S DEPARTURE

Garibaldi lived on Staten Island from October 1850 to April 1851. Barely nine months had passed, but they were months of extreme impatience, if not intolerance. One fine day, in keeping with his restless character, the longed-for and expected opportunity presented itself, after the search for work in the port and the concomitant humiliation. Resignation and a flat life did not fit into his indomitable character. The salvation, the liberation, was the arrival in New York of his idol and protector, Francesco Carpanetto, who had helped him during his long after Roman despair and the long wandering in exile between Gibraltar and Morocco, when he was rejected by all.

Garibaldi was freed from that stay which he accepted with difficulty, given his nature of action and great undertakings, his restless soul incapable of stasis and immobility. Despite Meucci's freedom and affection, he widely recognized that sedentary work of any kind was intolerable to him, including the making of candles for little money among other failed ventures.

Hence the cry of relief and release:

> My friend Francesco Carpanetto finally arrived in New York. From Genoa he had begun a large speculation for Central America. The *San Giorgio*, a ship belonging to him, had left Genoa with part of its cargo, and he himself had gone to England to prepare the rest and send it to Gibraltar, where the ship was to take it. Having decided that I would accompany him to Central America, we immediately made preparations for our departure, and in 51 I set out with Carpanetto for Chagres on an American steamer [the *Prometheus*] commanded by Captain Johnson. From Chagres we passed with a yacht of the same nation in San Juan of the North, and from there we took a dugout sailing up the same river of San Juan until the lake of Nicaragua. We crossed the lake and finally reached Granada, the most commercial port and town on the lake. In Granada we stayed a few days, kindly welcomed by some Italians established there, and there began the commercial operations of our friend Carpanetto,

for which we visited many parts of Central America, crossing the Isthmus of Panama several times. (Garibaldi 1888, 267).

This is how Phillip K. Cowie relates the American sojourn in extreme synthesis, but with a few more details:

> In January-February 1851 he worked at a small candle factory of his friend and guest on Staten Island, Antonio Meucci, a Florentine exile, inventor by profession and one of the first experimenters of the wire-transmission of sound. Garibaldi stayed there until the end of April 1851, when, under the false name of 'Joseph Anzani,' he left with two Genoese friends, Francesco Carpanetto and Edoardo Reta, for a business trip to Central America, visiting the Kingdom of Mosquito, Nicaragua, and El Salvador. It seems that their idea was to continue to California in order to buy at a good price some abandoned ships in the port of San Francisco. In Central America they lost track of the Hero, also because he continually changed his name in order to "avoid curiosity and police harassment," as he wrote in his memoirs. (Cowie 63)

Still Cowie reports a mysterious trip in November 1850:

> In November of the same year [1850] he embarked on the *Giorgia*, a steamer of the United States service, from New York to Havana and the Chagres River (Panama) and back. But it seems that his collaboration with the U.S. *Post Office* was brief: about a month. It was no longer continued, nothing is known as to why. (Cowie 63)

Regarding these Caribbean transfers, thanks to Anna Tola's research, two stops in Havana have been verified.[52]

---

[52] A stay in Jamaica remains unclear. According to Ghisalberti, it would prove a gift of Italians and citizens of that island, deposited at the Museo del Risorgimento in

Cowie himself, however, reports a hypothesis that he rejects: "In our time, an Italian writer, Salvatore Loi, reworked the story, writing about Garibaldi being in Havana to carry out a 'secret mission' aimed at inciting Cubans to revolution. Thus, we have a representation of the Hero that conforms to the militant and revolutionary figure of the man that each of us knows from historical traditions but that does not faithfully reflect the true aspects of his 'visit' to Cuba. Garibaldi was there for two 'weekends,' and it is known that he worked on a U.S. Postal Service steamer, the *Giorgia*. I would say that in four days one cannot organize a terrorist cell nor carry out a 'secret mission'" (Cowie 71).[53]

Jessie White Mario provides another synthetic sequence of the presence in New York: "The first years of his exile in America were very sad for our hero. Comforted only by the affection of friends and especially by the fraternal care of Antonio Meucci, he found an honorable job in the latter's manufacture of tallow candles. Later, an Italian-American company gave him the command of a ship destined to trade with Central America, but when he reached Panama, struck down by a pernicious fever, he had to stay ashore, and without the loving and intelligent care of Giovanni Basso he would probably have died there. In Panama he was very happy to see Carpanetti [sic] again, who had to give up his job as consul because he had hosted him in Tangier, and with him on the *San Giorgio* he left for Lima, where Don Pedro de Negri, a rich Genoese, offered him the command of a vessel laden with grains and silver. Three months I will give the voyage, during which he was much impressed by a dream, which he himself related, and which may be added to the collection of forebodings fulfilled" (White 423–427).

Palermo, the result of a subscription promoted by Armaboldi from Bergamo. In the letter of thanks Garibaldi offers to offer his sword in defense of peoples of any race.
[53] See also Salvatore Loi.

Regarding the passage to Nicaragua are interesting pieces of anti-clerical news reported by Phillip Cowie: "Garibaldi remained in Nicaragua for four months, until he had to leave the country hastily because of a coup d'état organized by the military and, it seems, also by the Bishop of León; it would have been more prudent for him to stay away for some time. He left for Peru because a ship, owned by his friend Carpanetto, was to arrive in the port of Callao in those days with a cargo from Europe for the main ports of the Pacific, Valparaiso, Lima, La Union, San Francisco, and they hoped to find it there, so they could then return to Central America, continue their business and possibly even go to California" (Cowie 63).

The reasons for these frantic transfers just after his arrival and in the health conditions he himself reported are obscure. He specified in his memoirs that he was not yet personally engaged in an activity of his own, yet it was the traveling, the moving from one place to another in the frenzy of adventure, that was the spring of his action, the fullness of his happiness, and the cause of satisfaction:

> I accompanied my friend in those excursions more as a traveling companion than as a collaborator in commerce, in which I confess myself a novice; but such was not Carpanetto, and I admired the activity and intelligence with which he handled every store that could produce advantages. I was traveling at that time under the name of Giuseppe Pane (Galeota Capece 651),[54] whom I had already hired in '34 to avoid the curiosity and harassment of the police. Carpanetto's commercial combinations were based on the arrival of the ship *San Giorgio* in Lima, and he

---

[54] Galeota Capece writes: "He left Chiavari, on September 16, 1849, with the intention of returning to the sea and earning his 'bread' (a term that became a convenient name for him — "Giuseppe Pane," in fact — and that appears, but not always, in the records).

planned to go to this city to wait for her.... On this last journey I was assailed by the terrible fevers endemic in that climate and in that country sown with swamps. They struck me like a thunderbolt and prostrated me; I was never so struck down by evil as at that time, and if I had not had the good fortune to find excellent Italians in Panama, including the two Monti brothers and various good Americans, I believe I would not have been freed from the disease. In that dangerous circumstance, my dear Carpanetto took truly fraternal care of me. Embarking in Panama on the English steamer that was to take us to Lima, the sea air was for me a balm that greatly refreshed me.... In Lima, where we found the *San Giorgio*, I had a splendid welcome from that rich and generous Italian colony, especially from the Sciutto, Denegri and Malagrida families. Mr. Pietro Denegri gave me the command of the *Carmen*, a boat of four hundred tons, and I prepared for a trip to China. (Garibaldi 1888, 267–68)

Denegri belonged to a wealthy family originally from Chiavari, then from Nice, and established in Peru; the *Carmen* was a clipper or mercantile freighter.

At last, he could return to his business and to the dream that tortured him in that inactivity, the yearning that followed him to have a ship of his own to steer, the need to sail the world. And such was the embarkation in October 1851 first for the Caribbean and Central America on the *San Giorgio*, the ship Carpanetto had led with a cargo from Genoa and then London.

Phillip K. Cowie writes: "Garibaldi's arrival at Callao, on October 5, 1851, was a splendid moment. The Italian republicans in Lima, knowing of his arrival, sent a delegation to the port to receive him and bring him triumphantly to the capital. At the end of the month, the unemployed Garibaldi was hired by a certain Don Pedro Denegri who gave him the command of one of his ships, the *Carmen*, an old brig bought shortly before in San Francisco. At the end of October, he received Peruvian citizenship and a Peruvian captain's license, things quite difficult to obtain for a foreigner, and probably obtained through the pressure of his acquaintances on the local government.... On January 10, 1852, Garibaldi left for China, captain of the ship *Carmen*. He arrived in Hong Kong on April 14, 1852; then he went to Canton and then to the port of Amoy on the northeast coast, where he sold his cargo of guano. He stayed there through the month of May, having the old ship repaired at the local dock. Amoy was China's most infamous port for its trade in Chinese slaves, the so-called 'coolies,' whom American and British merchants sent across the Pacific even to the plantations of Cuba. There, no doubt, Garibaldi saw hundreds of Chinese waiting for the ships to depart, all together like beasts, naked, with a 'P,' 'S' or 'C' printed on their chests: letters that signified their destination, respectively Peru, Sandwich Islands, California. Upon his return to Canton in June 1852, he met Englishman Anthony Enright, captain of the clipper *Chrysalite*, a very fast sailing ship carrying tea to England. The two spent nearly a month waiting for their respective merchant ships. They both attended the Club where all the foreign captains and merchants residing there went" (Cowie 63–65).

A ship flying the Peruvian flag with a crew of fifteen men embarked in the islands of Cincia, south of Lima, a cargo of guano, the precious dung of birds, collected in the quarries of *guaneras*, destined for China. Returning to Callao for the final arrangements of the long voyage on January 10, 1852, he sailed for Canton, where he arrived after about ninety-three days of travel with a favorable wind. "Arrived in Canton, my consignee sent me to Amoy, not finding an opportunity to sell the cargo of guano in the first piazza. From Amoy I returned to Canton, and the return cargo not being ready, I loaded for Manila different cargo. From Manila I returned to Canton, where we found them repairing the timbers of the *Carmen*, which had been broken, and changing the coppers. With the load ready, we left Canton for Lima" (Garibaldi 272).

In July Garibaldi left Canton with a cargo for Manila, from where he returned in August, carrying, among other things, mail and newspapers for Hong Kong. The cargo in Canton, consisting of textiles and chinoiserie, being ready, he left for Lima on September 4.

From the vagueness about the nature of the cargo and the doubts about what type it was, there is a short line to accusations of being a "negriero" advanced against Garibaldi given news that many Chinese emigrants, whose colonies were well established in North and South America, landed in Callao. The indefatigable and heroic navigator tortured by arthritis had and still has today praising worshippers and mortal enemies who consider the conquest of the Kingdom of the Two Sicilies a serious fault.

The question concerns above all the interpretation to be given to the opinion on Garibaldi pronounced by the shipowner Pietro Denegri who had entrusted him with the ship. It is derived from a conversation he had with the famous and greatest Italian writer of the sea Augusto Vittorio Vecchi (1842–1932), alias Jack La Bolina, and reported by him in the biography of Garibaldi.

As it happens in these cases the sin of manipulation and information is to extrapolate a sentence from the context and omit the rest. Therefore, to honor the truth we want to bring back the whole dialogue which took place in 1865, leaving the judgment to those free from spite. Referring to the "small manufacture of tallow candles," La Bolina indignantly pointed out:

> It is a great example that of Giuseppe Garibaldi who, once again a sailor, went to Lima and obtained from D. Pedro

Denegri of Chiavari the command of the clipper the Carmen and sailed from Callao to China transporting Chinese emigrants. 'Don Victor, I have never had a captain like him who spent so little on me,' said Don Pedro Denegri to me in 1865 in Lima, telling me about Garibaldi. But neither the cares of industry nor the responsibility of a merchant captain stifled the patriot and the general. Regarding a letter from Garibaldi to his father of September 19, 1853, he added: 'Such was the man, frank, industrious, courteous, naive as a child, impressionable and like a poet. And there were Italians who depicted him in their writings as a leader of wild bands, as an unleashed antichrist from hell!' 'He always brought me Chineses (coolies) in the number embarked and all fat and in good health; because he treated them like men and not like beasts.' Denegri said these words to me. Here is the fierce man! 'Never a complaint of sailors against him.' Behold the violent man!" (La Bolina, 94-97)

This favorable opinion would have arisen from the low mortality rate of the slaves transported, which generally reached 15 percent to 20 percent. I don't know how conceivable a traffic of Chinese is, those who were sold in Peru and employed in guano quarries (guaneras), even more so were they "exploited and day and night guarded by armed guards to prevent them from committing suicide."[55]

Removing all doubt about the nature of these Chinese is the research of Phillip K. Cowie: "For more than a century, this reference to 'Chinese' on board Garibaldi's vessel embarrassed his biographers and made his enemies jump for joy. With this uncontested information the latter were able to denigrate the figure of the Hero, calling him a 'negro' and a 'slaver,' since at the time of his visit to the East there existed between China and

---

[55] See Ignazio Coppola and Galeota Capece (663-664).

Peru an extensive traffic in slaves, the so-called 'coolies,' and Garibaldi, by his own declaration in the memoirs, went to the port of Amoy, of infamous reputation, as we have seen. The former, instead of seeking the truth, did not clarify the subject, perhaps for fear of being confronted with uncomfortable results. My research has shown, however, that Vecchi was very wrong. In Lima, Vecchi did not fully understand the local language used in Denegri's house and in his environment, a curious mixture of colonial Spanish, Genoese, Italian, and Quechua, the language of the Incas. 'The Chinese' for Denegri were Peruvian people of mixed blood, 'los chinos' in common parlance. Oriental slaves, on the other hand, were called 'colonos chinos,' an expression Denegri did not use when speaking with Vecchi.

"There is documentation that lists all the vessels that carried oriental slaves to Peru, but the name of Garibaldi's vessel does not appear in it [*Memoria que presenta a las camaras de 1853, Lima*, E. Aranda, 1853, appendix n° 16]. There is, also, a list of the goods Garibaldi brought from China [in the Limeño newspaper, *El comercio*, January 25, 1853, p. 2, col. 1]. But the myth of slaves aboard the Carmen dies hard, and biographers keep repeating the old wrong story" (Cowie 72).[56]

Considering the situation of the winds and skirting the unfavorable winds and tides of the torrid zone, passing through the Indian Sea with constant breezes from the east, for the Bass Strait, he sailed between New Zealand and Lord Aukland Land. While sailing in the Indian Ocean on March 19, 1852, he suffered the loss of his dear mother. Driven by strong westerly winds, he headed for the west coast of America. After one hundred days of prosperous navigation, he returned to Lima. In the last days there was a shortage of provisions, so he "put the people on ration for foresight." It wasn't all that simple, however, as Cowie

---

[56] My research on this subject was published in 1998.

reports:
> After twelve days of navigation, on September 16, 1852, still in the China Sea near the coast of the Philippines, the *Carmen* found herself involved in a terrible tidal wave (the city of Manila was destroyed that same day by a frightful earthquake), followed immediately by a typhoon of an intensity never seen before. Garibaldi, due to his usual reticence, unfortunately did not leave us any description of this typhoon [F. DABADIE, *Episode inédit de la via de Garibaldi*, in Revue Française, 10 juillet 1859]. François Dabadie, a Frenchman living in Lima, later spoke with the man who was the second aboard the *Carmen*, perhaps Giovanni Battista Fontanarosa, and left us a terrifying description. (Cowie 66)

On his return from China in the port of Callao, he was met in the roadstead by the Sardinian consul, who informed him of the death of his mother, Maria Rosa Nicoletta Raimondi (22 January 1776–20 March 1852).[57] For this reason, which deeply affected him, and probably also for political news, Garibaldi hastened his return.

"They disembarked the cargo in Lima, and left in ballast [in seafaring slang, 'without payload'] for Valparaíso, where upon arriving, they chartered the *Carmen* for a trip from Chile to Boston with copper. We landed at various ports on the Chile coast. ... We finished our cargo with wool over copper at Islay (Peru). Leaving Islay [May 25, 1853], we sailed at noon for Cape Horn, and after a very stormy crossing, in the high latitudes, reached Boston" (Garibaldi 1888, 273–274).

In that "substantial strip of Italy," which grew up around the primitive Ligurian colony that landed there toward the end of the eighteenth century, in splendid Valparaíso, the largest

---

[57] From Loano, she was a daughter of fishermen; his father Domenico Garibaldi (1766–1841), originally from Chiavari, owned the tartana Santa Reparata. Giuseppe was the second born of six children.

maritime and mercantile city in Chile, Garibaldi felt at home. All the Italians ran to meet him and offered him a magnificent flag that then followed him across the Atlantic and flew in "Quarto, Palermo, and the Volturno river." In fact, the "flag of the Italians," donated by the Italians of Valparaíso was delivered to him in Caprera in 1855. The "Flag of the Thousand," in the hands of the standard-bearer Giuseppe Campo, guided the Thousand from Quarto to Calatafimi where, on May 15, it was defended by the captain of the Genoese Navy, Simone Schiaffino, who died on the hill of "il Pianto dei Romani."

The great adventure from Chile to Boston had ended with the return to its starting point. It seemed that other crossings awaited him, toward other exotic destinations, for hundreds of days, forecasting winds and storms, but the hope of having found the way to trade and to command a ship had vanished. "From Boston I had orders to go to New York, where upon arrival I received a letter with some reproaches from the owner of the *Carmen*, which seemed to me undeserved, so I left the command of the ship." He had taken advantage of all the opportunities of the ports without ever leaving the ship without cargo, yet something had gone wrong. Garibaldi does not specify the subject of the reproaches but tries to advance his own opinion on the discontent of the ship owner: "I must add on the account of Don Pedro Denegri, master of the *Carmen*, that I was treated by him with great kindness throughout the time I had the fortune to serve him. But a parasitic Tersite, who had insinuated himself into the company, tried to make me look bad with the chief" (Garibaldi 1888, 274–275).

It is probable that he spent a few days on Staten Island, although he says simply "New York," with Meucci, Foresti, Avezzana, and the English colonel Hugh Forbes, another of the faithful who had followed him after his retreat from Rome in 1849: "I stayed a few more days in New York, enjoying the dear company of my precious friends Foresti, Avezzana, and Pastacaldi." Then on January 12, 1854, he left the United States forever: "With money earned in the Pacific and with a small inheritance made in Nice, Garibaldi returned to Italy in 1854" (La Bolina 97). "When Captain Figari arrived in the harbor with the intention of buying a ship, I had a proposal from him to command it and take it to Europe. I accepted, and we went with Captain Figari to Baltimore, where the *Commonwealth* ship was purchased; loaded with flour and grain, I sailed for London, where I arrived in February '54."

In New York, the consul Tagliacarne expressed to him in a conversation the conviction that the time was ripe for a return to his homeland, a sentiment that was not exactly mirrored later by Cavour. His old friend Figari had the task of purchasing a ship destined to transport coal on behalf of Genoese ship owners, the always present "Ligurian rigmarole." In command of the *Commonwealth*, purchased with his assistance, he sailed for England.

In London he met Mazzini, who wrote about Garibaldi's return and mentioned the possibility of sending him to Sicily. "In London he was welcomed with honors and deference: a beautiful picture of him in 'morning coat' and black tie remains." For the return home lacked the formal consent of the Sardinian government. The Sardinian ambassador, D'Azeglio, Massimo's nephew, wrote to Cavour, who replied: "If he comes to see his family's business, fine, but if he comes to do Mazzini's business, we won't let him stay even for a minute." The last voyage was made still in command of the ship that had brought him from New York. And so he arrived in Genoa, as Dilani writes: "At home, at last" (Galeota Capece 665).

Of great importance is the news reported by journalist Jessie White Mario, who gives the pulse on the situation of oppression and intolerance of immigrants: "He left for New York with De

Negri's assignment to take over the command of the *Commonwealth*, and he witnessed the disdain of the American citizenship, shared by the Germans living there, for the recent deportation of Italian exiles, a disdain that grew when they learned of the bad treatment inflicted on those wretches during the trip. A meeting was called and presided over by Foresti to solemnly welcome his compatriots to the land of liberty. And since the Piedmontese government had preceded these unfortunates by the most atrocious slanders, collected and disseminated by the *New York Echo*, a committee of American, English, and Italian citizens was appointed in the persons of Dwight Hagg, Colonel Forbes, Garibaldi's former officer, and Foresti himself, in order to learn about the cause of exile for each one and to report to the Society of Friends of Civil and Religious Liberty in order to find employment and provide work for the needy. They invited Garibaldi to take part as vice-president at a great meeting fixed for September 22, and he answered by letter of September 14, 1853, that he was leaving for Boston and would be back on that date, but he applauded the proposed demonstration, in order to approve the conduct of the good and generous Ingraham" (Mario 428).

    This long voyage around the world's seas brought about a profound change in Garibaldi's soul: "To his old republican friends in New York he spoke of peace and tried to get them to agree because they were all brothers of the same big family even if they were separated by ideological struggles: 'Having found (very frequent) dissensions among the Italians, I allowed myself to convey conciliation.'"

    Garibaldi tried to convince everyone that in order to "create Italy" it was not necessary to resort to small unpopular revolutions of Mazzini's type, but that the hopes of Italy were placed in Piedmont. In a letter to Giuseppe Valerio he wrote: "About the idea manifested to you of conciliations among the Italians, I have written to various of the most influential people proposing for a program to unite around the Italian flag of Piedmont whatever has been the conviction of the system for the past, and frankly, having no other goal than that of reuniting Italy to that government, fighting all the foreigners who oppress it. I will propagate the same idea elsewhere, to as many as possible, so convinced am I of the wisdom of this" (Garibaldi 1981, 55–56).

In London on May 6, he met Mazzini and the great Russian writer and revolutionary Aleksandr Herzen. "So convinced am I of the wisdom of this" he tried to convince Mazzini about the new way to deal with the great problem of the unification of Italy. So, he had written to him on February 26 in London: "Leaning on the Piedmont government is a little hard, I understand, but I believe it the best party and that it will amalgamate to that center all the different colors that divide us; however it happens, whatever the cost. Knit the tracks to the greater piece of the log" (Garibaldi 1981, 62).

Mazzini was thinking of a revolutionary expedition to Sicily, and from this moment their friendship soured.

We continue again with Garibaldi's account in this chapter of exile: "From London I went to Newcastle, where we loaded coal for Genoa, and reached the latter port on May 10 of the same year. At Genoa, being ill with rheumatism, I was transported to the house of my friend Captain G. Paolo Augier, where I received kind hospitality for fifteen days; then I passed to Nice, where I had the good fortune to finally hold my children to my breast after a five-year exigency. The period from my arrival in Genoa in May '54 until my departure from Caprera in February 1859 is of no interest. I spent it partly sailing and partly cultivating a small property I purchased on the Island of Caprera."

Mario informs us of these last glorious stages before returning to Italy: "In April 1854, he arrived in Newcastle on Tyne, where he received a large and cordial welcome from

Joseph Cowen or from the workers of the city, whose every act and fact was already known by the mouth of Mazzini. But he refused any public demonstration, so it was decided by the Friends of European Freedom to present him with a sword and a telescope, the result of a public subscription of no more than ten cents per signature. In a short time, a large sum was raised, and on April 11, on board his own ship, he was presented with the sword and telescope with the inscription: 'To General Garibaldi from the people of Tynside the Friends of European Liberty. Newcastle on Tyne, April 1854.'"

In his letter of thanks, the general wrote: "Born and educated in the cause of humanity, my heart is wholly given to liberty, to universal freedom, now and forever. England is a great and powerful nation. Independent of all, in the vanguard of progress, the enemy of despotism, the only refuge of the exile, the friend of the oppressed. Your government has given autocracy a checkmate, the Austrians a lesson. The despots of Europe are consequently against you. If ever in any circumstance my arm can be useful to you, I will be happy to draw the beautiful sword given to me."

And we close with the final leg of this second exile: "He arrived in Genoa with a load of coal, and finding himself the possessor of modest holdings, he had no heart to depart again from his country and his children; so that, having retired to Nice, we see him there leading a simple and reserved life. The conditions of the parties had totally changed. The star of Piedmont was rising; that of the republicans, inasmuch as the movement of February 6 for the dissolution, after the imprisonment of Petroni, of the republican committee of Rome, and for the last attempt of Lunigiana, had waned."

La Bolina added other details: "In Genoa he found friends, not least the brothers Orlando, Sicilian exiles who gave him in command the *Salvatore*, a small propeller ship that trafficked from Genoa to Marsilia touching Nice. This small ship was a hair's breadth away from serving a very noble undertaking to which Garibaldi had offered himself, that is, to free Settembrini and his companions from a life sentence on Ponza. How this did not come to be is reported by Settembrini in *Ricordanze*." He gave Meucci the red shirt he had worn during and after the Rome campaign. He also left him a dagger and a cameo engraved with his image, a life-size portrait of him, a pair of pistols, and a mirror in front of which he used to trim his blond beard. All these objects can be found in the Staten Island cottage that has become a museum. This is where chapter 10 of his memoirs, titled "Esiglio," ends.

On December 29, 1855, with the inheritance of 35 thousand lire from his mother (who had died on March 20, 1852) and from his brother Felice he bought a parcel of the land on Caprera that included a shepherd's house. Later, with the help of thirty friends, he built a farm; and in 1865, through donations of friends, he became the owner of the entire island, which he called his friend Colonel Giovanni Froscianti (1811-1885) to administer.

Everything else is another story, as he himself would say.

THE HOST OF THE GARIBALDI-MEUCCI MUSEUM AND LINCOLN

At the outbreak of the American War of Secession in 1861, President Abraham Lincoln attempted to recruit Garibaldi to join the Union Army and invited him to serve as a major general. Garibaldi said he would serve under two conditions: first, that slavery would be permanently abolished; and second, that he would be given full command of the army. Both conditions were impossible for Lincoln to accept, and the offer was quietly withdrawn. However, Garibaldi and Italy were honored by the participation in the Civil War of a regiment of volunteers recruited in 1865 in the district of New York called the "Garibaldi Guard" and composed of many Italian immigrants, Garibaldians and Mazzinians.

Monument to Giuseppe Garibaldi by Giovanni Turini, 1888

Washington Square Park, Lower Manhattan
Postmortem

Memories and Celebrations

The extent to which the excellence of his life and his presence in that place of exile, now his permanent home, was recognized by Italian Americans and others is proven by the fact that just a few days after his death, in the meadow in front of the cottage, a memorial stone was erected with the inscription: Antonio Meucci — The Inventor of The Telephone. On the right were images of two examples of the telephone, from 1854 and 1864, and the wiring diagrams of the most important models. At the top of the memorial stone, a death mask of Meucci was placed inside a laurel wreath.

As a Freemason awarded the 33rd degree of the Ancient and Accepted Scottish Rite, Meucci had the opportunity and honor to preside in New York on August 8, 1888, by proxy of the Grand Master of the Grand Orient of Italy Adriano Lemmi, over the ceremony of honorary initiation of the Italian ambassador to the United States with a speech of welcome and good wishes.

Hometown Monuments

1. A tombstone in the house where he was born in Florence in via De' Serragli, 44:

Qui Nacque
Il 13 Aprile 1808
Antonio Meucci
Inventore del Telephone
I suoi cittadini posero il 16 Maggio 1996.

2. A bronze plaque in the headquarters of "L'urne dei forti" in the Basilica of Santa Croce that reads:

FAR FROM THE HOMELAND ON THE ATLANTIC SHORE THAT FIRST ANOTHER FLORENTINE TOUCHED WITH THE TELEPHONE THE INSTRUMENT THAT CANCELS TODAY EVERY DISTANCE BETWEEN MEN AND PEOPLES;

3. A plaque on Palazzo delle Poste e dei Telegrafi in Florence on June 15, 1924, in via Pellicceria that reads:

ANTONIO MEUCCI INVENTOR OF THE TELEPHONE DIED IN MDCCCLXXXIX IN A FOREIGN LAND POOR AND DEFRAUDED OF HIS RIGHTS. VITTORIO VENETO'S ITALY AND HER FLORENCE CLAIM WITH MATERNAL PRIDE THE GLORY.
THE ITALIAN ASSOCIATION FOR THE CULT OF NATIONAL MEMORIES COMMEMORATES ON THIS XV GIUGNO MCMXXIV**

4. An identical plaque offered by the City of Florence in the courtyard of the ancient Teatro Tacón, in the headquarters of his workshop.

5. The Italian Post Office issued a commemorative Marconi and Meucci stamp on the occasion of the first centenary of the International Telecommunication Union (ITU) in 1965.

6. On May 28, 2002, there was held a Meucci Day celebration ceremony by the Ministry of Telecommunications.

7. On November 7, 2012, by the will of the heirs of the engineer Basilio Catania, the Meucci- Catania Archive allowed Catania to obtain from Congress the complete rehabilitation of Meucci as "inventor of the telephone" which records were moved to the Marconi Foundation of Villa Griffone.

8. The celebration of the 150th Anniversary of Meucci's "talking telegraph" took place in Havana (Cuba), November 19–25, 1999, in the framework of the IV Week of Italian Culture in Cuba, more than a thousand people in the Basilica Menor de San Francisco de Asís attended.

9. A postage stamp bearing Meucci's image.

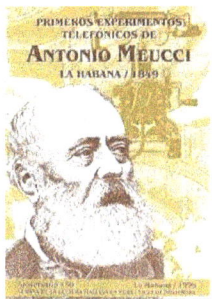

10. The unveiling of the plaque at the side of the main entrance of the Gran Teatro de Tacón.

NEW YORK MONUMENTS

1. A monument to Antonio Meucci at the Garibaldi-Meucci Museum was inaugurated on September 16, 1923. It was erected on the initiative of Captain Cuomo Cerulli by the Italian Community residing in the United States and supported by General Guglielmotti and with contributions from public and private entities. It was sculpted by Ettore Ferrari with marble offered by the City of Rome, with bronze from the Austrian cannons captured in Vittorio Veneto, offered by the Ministry of War, transported there by ship. Under the bust of the monument rest in an urn his ashes, guarded by a Garibaldian. Francesco Moncada was the official speaker at the ceremony of the commemoration of Meucci's birth, on April 14, 1932.

2. The Stone Meucci Memorial, "Father of the Telephone" in the small garden of Meucci Square in the populous neighborhood of Bensonhurst (Brooklyn, USA), placed on April 10, 1989, by the Italian American Historical Society and cared for by it. The New York City resolution to name the Brooklyn triangle at the intersection of 12th Street West with 86th Street and Avenue U after Meucci was signed on March 26, 1940, by Fiorello La

Guardia, the mayor of New York at the time. The Stone Memorial with the inscription: Antonio Meucci — 1808-1889, was laid by the Italian American Historical Society on April 9, 1989.

3. Monument to Giuseppe Garibaldi, bronze statue, 3 m high, by Giovanni Turini, unveiled June 4, 1888, six years after his death in Washington Square Park, Lower Manhattan. It was again the well-deserving Italian monumental celebrant Carlo Barsotti (1850-1927), who launched the fundraising campaign in his newspaper *Il progresso italo-americano* (1879) but lacked funds and the project remained unfinished due to Turini's death in 1899. The planned move to Staten Island did not take place either. It became the place of worship for Italian exiles. Since the 1960s, the freshmen of New York University have thrown a penny at the base of the statue in the hope of good luck. In 1970, when it was moved east to create a driveway, a glass jar was found with newspaper clippings reporting in Italian the death of Garibaldi on June 4, 1882.

Barsotti, founder of the *Italian American Bank*, was the promoter of the contested statues of Christopher Columbus in Columbus Circle (1892), of Giuseppe Verdi (1906), of Giovanni da Verrazzano in bronze in Battery Park, the work of Palermo-born Ettore Ximenes (1855-1926) on the occasion of the Hudson-Fulton celebration (1909), of Dante Alighieri in Dante Park (1921).

4. Playground in Brooklyn, Garibaldi playground: NYC Department of Parks and Recreation. From the NYC Parks website: Garibaldi playground (this text is part of Parks Historical Signs Project and can be found posted within the park). We read, in fact, the following on the NYC Parks website:

> "This playground was named for Italian patriot and leader Giuseppe Garibaldi (1807-1882) by a local law passed by the City Council and signed by Mayor Edward I. Koch in 1985. The naming was initiated by the Italian Historical Society of America as a tribute to Garibaldi as well as to the strong Italian

heritage that is shared by many Brooklynites, especially residents of Bensonhurst.

Giuseppe Garibaldi was a crusader for the unification of an independent Italy....

[...] Subsequently Garibaldi went to the United States where he lived for four years in exile in Clifton, Staten Island, recovering from arthritis and earning his living by making candles. This site is marked by the Garibaldi-Meucci Museum on Tompkins Avenue....

[...] Garibaldi's international reputation was such that President Abraham Lincoln offered him a command in the Union Army at the beginning of the Civil War in 1861. Garibaldi declined, choosing to remain in Italy in order to participate in further military campaigns.

This property, located in Bensonhurst on 18th Avenue between 82nd and 83rd Streets, was acquired by Parks in 1937. The granite monument was installed here on October 3, 1990, by the Italian Historical Society of America in honor of Garibaldi. Another monument to the 'George Washington of Italy' was sculpted by Giovanni Turini and erected in Washington Square Park in 1888.[58]

ORIGINALITY AND VARIETY OF PATENTS

Meucci's inventiveness and creativity had no limits, and he tried on every daily occasion, or in the difficulty of the proposed or occasional problems, to find the best solution to make use of the instruments easy and simple. About twenty-two patents are cited regarding chemical or mechanical solutions, the official ones of which he was owner and depositary. But perhaps they are a little more.

---

[58] The New York City Parks Department website states that Garibaldi lived in the United States for four years (https://www.nycgovparks.org/parks/garibaldi-playground/highlights/19654). He did not. He lived on and off in the United States during the two-year period 1850-1852.

Therefore, we give here a chronological list, leaving the specificities and particularities to the aficionados and the experts. We give only the main prototypes in the vast range of applications and modulations of the invention of telephone models, which cover his entire life from the first theatrical approaches in Florence to the dominant theme of the entire American stay, and for which he is famous and acclaimed in every part of the world.

1859. Candle patent and in Clifton the New York Paraffine Candle Co. factory, capable of producing one thousand stearic candles per day. They were marketed by Rider & Clark of New York. Legend has it that Lumiere used them in Beauty and the Beast. The discovery of oil in Pennsylvania and the use of kerosene decreased the candle business.

1860. At the request of Enrico Bendelari, a coral trader in New York, he developed a process to bleach red coral, making it a more valuable pink color.

That same year, he studied the applications of his dry cell battery to electric traction and "to other branches of industry."

1862. At the request of a Havana merchant, he invented a special burner for kerosene lamps of wide use, equipped with two metal tips that, developing electricity in contact with the flame, made it clear and smokeless, avoiding the use of the usual glass tube (U.S. Patent No. 36,192).

1863. Patent for oils for painting, obtained from kerosene.

1864. Proposed to the American Army during the war of secession, and to Garibaldi in view of the third war of independence of Italy, a new type of ammunition for rifles and cannons from the campaign, of his own invention, which produced greater destruction of the target, as he described them in a letter to Garibaldi, preserved in the Museo Centrale del Risorgimento in Rome.

In anticipation of this third war of Italian independence, a

Permanent Central Committee was created in New York for the formation of a corps of volunteers to be sent to Italy, and Meucci was appointed its president.

1865. Paper pulp from wood / vegetables. Vegetable wicks.

1867. Patent for sheets of algae paper, white and durable, which he was to exploit commercially for the use of newspapers, and especially daily newspapers, as a defense against the city's constant rains and wrinkling. To exploit the royalties from the patent on the manufacture of this algae paper, in 1867 he founded the "Perth Amboy Fiber Company" in Perth Amboy, New Jersey, with American capital and Meucci as superintendent. Among the first in the world, it carried out the recycling of wastepaper and the recovery of the leachate. He designed a paper mill to be set up in Africa, with a detailed cost analysis.

1871. During the hospitalization and subsequent long convalescence for burns suffered in the explosion of the boiler of the *Westfield* ferry, which connected the harbor to Staten Island, having been recommended a diet based on fruit and abundant liquids, he invented and then patented a particular process of manufacturing a nutritious and pleasant drink. I think of our hydrolitine, Alka seltzer, an effervescent and sparkling drink based on fruit and vitamins, healthy for the healing of severe burns reported (US Patent No. 122.478).

Another idea that is still widely accepted in our tastes and consumption was the different seasonings for pasta and other foods, based on the input and commission of Roberto Merloni, at the time General Manager of Star, Agrate – Milan (US Patent No. 142.071). For direct marketing he opened a small restaurant of Made in Italy products, a challenge to hot dogs with "lampredotto," "pappa di pomodoro," and "caponata."

1873. Deposited caveat, renewed in 1874 and extended to Canada, on the study of a steamship with propeller propulsion, suitable for canal navigation, in view of the passage of the two Oceans in the Panama Canal. Meat ragout patent.

1874. Deposited caveat on refining mineral oils, with a view to commercialization at the time of the explosion of large oil well drilling around the 1860s. In response to market demands, he studied on the production of plastic materials.

1875. Patent of milk meter that anticipated by fifteen years the Babcock Test, from the name of the developer Stephen M. Babcock (1843–1931), professor at the University of Wisconsin, bottle and test, invented in 1890, to determine, in an economic and practical way, the fat content in milk with a special bottle, useful to detect adulterations of producers, diluting milk with water or skimming cream.

1876. At the request of the industrialist Giuseppe Tagliabue, he built aneroid barometers with terracotta figures of various shapes. Tagliabue, an immigrant, was in New York around 1834 and made and sold instruments such as barometers, thermometers, and hygrometers. It was registered in his name with Patent n. 111.885, dated February 14, 1871: "construction of an areometer or hydrometer with a scale which, when the instrument is applied to a must of unfermented grain, would directly indicate the percentage of spirits that may have been expected from said mash provided fermentation is brought to an appropriate point, and will admit a ready correction for excessive or defective fermentation without the necessity of complex calculations, or any reference to tables."

Conception and construction of a primitive hygrometer, represented in the figurine of a Gambrinus who, when the weather changes, raises or lowers a cup.

1878. Filing of caveats on methods of noise prevention in elevated railroads, a nagging problem in New York, where they ran very close to homes.

1880. Filing of Patent Application No. 13,140, for a copper braided telephone conductor and another for a telephone connecting warships and torpedoes guided by wire, serving water as a return conductor; disclosed a variant thereof for military uses on land.

1881. Filing of caveats on stamps and revenue stamps with their manufacturing process.

Patent of oils for varnishes and paints as per Commercial Circular in four languages for the sale of patent varnish "for the use of colors and to preserve wood from corruption and prevent insects from corroding it" (155).

A piano factory.

Patent of an "Acid Candle," sold for a few thousand dollars.

THE GARIBALDI - MEUCCI MUSEUM TODAY

The Garibaldi-Meucci Museum (Garibaldi Memorial)

The house where Antonio Meucci lived from 1850 to 1889 and Garibaldi from 1850 to 1854, originally known as the Garibaldi Memorial, was restored and became the Garibaldi-Meucci Museum in 1962. Located at 420 Tompkins Avenue at Chestnut Avenue in Staten Island, it is a typical American cottage on a small street parallel to the coast, overlooking the Atlantic. It had been bequeathed in the owner's will as a significant part of Italian American culture and history.

In 1881, having been sold to a brewery that had bought the adjoining lots, the cottage was moved to the east side of Forest Street but kept the orientation intact. In 1907 it was moved again to the corner of Chestnut Avenue at 420 Tompkins Avenue.

As can be seen in the drawing of the cottage and nearby Clifton Brewery building painted by Nestore Corradi in 1858, the larger building to the left first housed the stearic candle factory and later, in 1856, the Clifton Brewery, as seen by the inscription, and also a small piano factory.

Today it is owned and administered by the National Order Sons and Daughters of Italy Foundation, of the New York Grand Lodge. On April 17, 1980, it was added to the National Register of Historic Places and declared a New York State Monument and a U.S. National Monument.

The objects that belonged to Garibaldi during his stay and that had been included by Meucci in his will as historical finds of his stay in America were sold at auction at his death at ludicrously low prices: seven lire for the bed on which he had slept for years, two and twenty-five lire for the washbasin and so on. These items later were patiently searched for and repurchased.

The House Museum is a mausoleum of memories that arouses feelings of pride in being Italian; visiting is a true pilgrimage. During the ferry crossing one has a view of the skyline of New York City as seen in postcards, with the symbols of New York Harbor and the backdrop of the Statue of Liberty. No less exciting can be the passage across the monumental bridge of the first Florentine Verrazzano, the Verrazzano Narrows Bridge, one mile from the museum, with its reminders of the Italian spirit. It is surprising to recall the date, shortly after the discovery of Columbus, when another Italian entered that bay and was surrounded by its legitimate inhabitants with festive and incomprehensible exultations, which he astonished with trinkets or the firing of a gun. The bridge appears to us immense with its balustrades and the many darting cars.

We are greeted at the museum entrance by the words "Garibaldi and Meucci, an American friendship. Here lived in exile from 1851 to 1853 Giuseppe Garibaldi, the hero of two worlds," a title he shares with the Marquis of La Fayette, general of the American and French revolutions. D'Annunzio and Mussolini will steal from him the nickname of "duce," a literal translation from the Latin *dux*, meaning "commander." Then, stretching out before our eyes is the green lawn of the garden in front, and on the right, we enter the monumental complex commemorating Meucci, enclosed by a flower bed including the mausoleum tomb holding the ashes of the inventor and his wife, sculpted by Ettore Ferrini and erected in 1923. The building features a neo-Gothic façade and roofs rigidly sloping to withstand heavy winter snowfalls. The house in plans represents typical styles of the first half of the nineteenth century. The museum illustrates with photographs, memories, and documents the stay of Giuseppe Garibaldi and the unfortunate story of Meucci.

On the ground floor there are two rooms, one dedicated to each man. In Meucci and Ester's corner, there are many prototypes of teletrophones (one with wooden drums on which the copper coils were wound), many prints, pages of technical reports, and documentation of the process, as well as the inventor's funeral mask (modeled by the sculptor G. Turini), his rocking chair, and the pianola he built. Of Garibaldi's stay memories are preserved of this desolate and painful "second exile"—difficult both on account of the torment of rheumatism and due to the lasting, deep misery. On the upper floor one finds the bedroom where he rested in those few days after the unfortunate adventure of the Roman Republic and the loss of his beloved companion, when, to make a living, he adapted to making candles in Meucci's small business. Many artifacts and memorabilia, the symbols of his fight for freedom, are displayed, including two of his famous red shirts, two caps, three rifles, two pipes, eyeglasses, a chair, mirrors, a beautiful hat, a cane, frescoes, various honors, a series of photos of his monuments around the world and of tombstones and piazzas named for and dedicated to him, as well as photographs and historical documents of his stay in those few years.

Piano in the Music Room

It is a moving place of memory, an emotional testimony to the hard season of many exiled volunteers, strenuous fighters for independence and freedom, and of many victims of despotism who escaped hanging or shooting, and also other various innocent victims of emigration in the painful escape from daily misery and pellagra in the hope of an El Dorado promised and achieved by very few.

The management is reorganizing the exhibition space and reviewing the archive, but a planned highlight will be the installation of a new sculpture by the Venetian artist Giorgio Bortoli, forging a cultural link with Venice in honor of the Italians who reside on the island and make up 55 percent of its population.

Garibaldi's red shirt, guns, and other paraphernalia in his bedroom

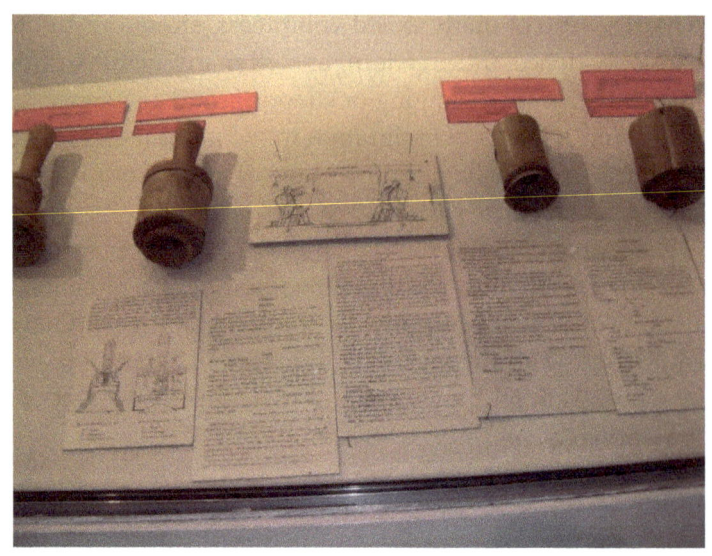

Meucci's Teletrophone

FROM THE PAST TO TODAY'S GLORIOUS TWINNING

Staten Island's extraordinary union of two Italian geniuses—the inventor of the telephone and the hero of two worlds—is set to become a perfect symbiosis with an extraordinary and unprecedented twinning, fostered by an act of love. On Friday, July 16, 2021, the Garibaldi Meucci Museum (represented by Joseph Sciame and Carl Ciaccio) connected directly with Venice, and a "passing of the baton" was sealed between the Lagoon City and Staten Island. This consisted of an embrace between two symbols of power, Manhattan's Metropolitan Life Tower, and the 98.6-meter-high St. Mark's bell tower. The New York tower was built in 1909 in the image of the Venetian Campanile, with its 213 meters in 53 stories marking a record in height that was surpassed in 1913 by the Woolworth Building.

Tower of Light

To initiate this Venice–New York union, the anniversary of the Campanile's collapse at 9:47 AM on July 14, 1902, was commemorated in St. Mark's Square. A stage was set up in the Loggetta di Sansovino, which also had been destroyed and is now made available by the Procuratoria di San Marco and crossed by scythes of lights drawing the Italian and US flags. On that terrible morning in 1902, the bell tower sank with a deafening roar and dissolved into dust, rubble, glass, and bricks, creating the effect that fog had descended. The episode appears to us today as almost a premonition of New York City's World Trade Center/Twin Towers' collapse in 2001. On April 23, 1903, a little less than a year after the Venetian tower fell, the cornerstone was laid for plans and promises made to rebuild it "where it was and as it was," although this did not happen until April 25, 1912.

At the height of the COVID outbreak, Venice wanted to assume leadership of the cultural project of restoring the Campanile (which is known affectionately by Venetians as "El Paron de Casa," or the master of the house), beginning with the "tochetòn," which is the largest chunk of the four-ton bell tower that was saved and guarded by Salvatore Arib and preserved later by his descendant Abraham Naum. This preservation is a historical example of Venetian resilience, from collapse to reconstruction, and a permanent symbol of rebirth.

In parallel with this historical re-enactment of the tower's collapse, an original artistic monument was projected on a screen, christened the "architructure" by Professor Marino Folin because it represents the "overcoming of divisions between the arts,"[59] and named the Tower of Light. Of all the works created by Venetian artist Giorgio Bortoli, in which he incorporates relics from the collapsed bell tower, the Tower of Light is the most beautiful and evocative work precisely because of its complexity. The "Two Towers" joined together in a single body is something he has worked on for years as a means of envisioning a symbol of friendship and cultural and artistic exchange between the two islands, Venice and Staten Island, the latter representing all of New York City.

Bortoli rebuilt the ancient bell tower at Marghera in 1999

---

[59] Prof. Folin stated: "In this case, sculpture and architecture; because of the symbolic nature of the work, which by representing the bell tower of St. Mark's enclosed within New York's Metropolitan Life Tower, is meant to express the synthesis of Europe and America in Western culture; and because of the quality and variety of materials, including glass, steel and even bricks from the ancient bell tower of St. Mark's collected by the author on the bottom of the Adriatic off the Lido: the materials also hold an allegorical significance in themselves and remind us of what recent studies have revealed, namely, that most likely before Columbus, Venetian ships had reached the Atlantic coast of North America" (12).

as a symbol and message of hope for the future; it represents a permanent expression of rebirth, which both encompasses and triumphs as a "restart" after the distressing COVID years. The majestic "archistructure" is a mix of architecture and sculpture, topped with a gold-plated angel and with the inscription indicating that the structure "represents the bell tower of St. Mark's contained within the Metropolitan Life Tower" in Manhattan, the latter having been patterned after the Venetian Campanile as if to transplant the symbol of old maritime Europe onto American soil.

Twelve meters high and weighing about 1,800 kilograms, the "archistructure" mixes two types of precious minerals, modern stainless steel, and classic Murano glass, as well as bronze and brick from the old bell tower, and 500 tiles illuminated by an LED light system. The plaque at the base reads: "The play of light from steel on bronze on glass and inside the bell tower of St. Mark's is designed to arouse sensations of movement like the palaces reflected at night in the water of the canals of Venice."

After being temporarily installed at various points in the Veneto region — from Aviano, the former USAF Air Force base, to the Venetian suburb of Concordia Sagittaria, and after stopping at Marco Polo Airport and crossing the Grand Canal in glory to the Biennale headquarters—in 2022 this admirable structure left Italy as a gift of good wishes to the Garibaldi Meucci Museum in Staten Island, which in turn was ready to welcome it on the front lawn of the small villa where the two geniuses had lived. Giorgio Bortoli stated: "With this sculpture I would like to unite my city with New York, in a twinning that also serves to foster cultural relations. A philosopher once spoke of 'aspiration to great heights,' which drives us to climb every tower, to satisfy our curiosity. Mankind has always connected spirituality with heights; we catch a glimpse of God,

Paradise is in the heavens. These are conceptions that man has always possessed within, against all rationality and as if they were imprinted in his genetic code, conceptions that we find in the principles of many religions" (9).

Prof. Massimo Cacciari at the outset of the project wrote: "Dear Bortoli, I had the opportunity to see the illustration of your 'Venice New York Project: the Two Towers,' and I wish to express my appreciation for the truly original idea. Between the American metropolis and the Lagoon City there are 'select affinities' that often, even if unjustifiably, escape the eyes of the most superficial observers of the architectural, urban planning, and social and economic history of large cities, in their dimensions of the present as well as of the past. I therefore congratulate you for an initiative that, symbolically, wants to make people reflect on such a misunderstood aspect. I appreciate your project because it is meant to be a 'cultural provocation' to Venice, which in the past was able to realize the ideal dream of a bridge city between the West and the East and today is no longer able to express its semantic role as a symbolic city. The 'Venice New York Project: The Two Towers' deservedly represents the ambition of wanting to bring the center of attention to Venice, a cosmopolitan city, and an authentic cultural capital" (11).

BIBLIOGRAPHY

Alexander Graham Bell's Family Papers (1865–1920). Library of Congress.

Andueza, José Maria de. 1841. *Isla de Cuba: pintoresca, histórica, política, literaria, mercantil e industrial*. Madrid: Boix.

Antonio Meucci: A Life for Science and for Italy. in radiomarconi.com.

Antonio Meucci. Il mago di Clifton. Enrico Guazzoni, Dir. Sabaudia Film.

Barzini, Luigi. 1926. "Una rivendicazione – Chi inventò il telefono?" *Il Corriere d'America* (7-14 21-28 February - 7-14 March) - New York.

Bell, Alexander Graham. 1865-1910. "Entry, March 10, 1876." *Notebooks* 1-18. archive.org/details/AlexanderGrahamBells Notebooks.

Bell, Alexander Graham. 1876. "Improvement in Telephony." *Letter Patent Number 174,465*. (February 14): 1-4. granted Mar. 7, 1876, USPTO. A. G. Bell, *Improvement in Electric Telegraphy, U.S.* Patent No. 186787, filed Jan. 15, 1877, granted Jan. 30, 1877, USPTO.

Bell, Alexander Graham. 1922. "Prehistoric Telephone Days." *National Geographic Magazine* 41.3 (March): 223-241.

Bianchi, Umberto. 1923. *La rivendicazione di una Gloria Italiana* — (Antonio Meucci). Rome: Tipografia Camera dei Deputati.

Biblioteca del Liceo de la Habana. Vol 1 (1946): 7.

Bonavía, Leopoldo Fornés. 2003. *Cuba, cronologia, cinco siglos de historia, politica y cultura*. Madrid: Editorial Verbum.

Bonfiglio, Giovanni. 1993. *Los italianos en la sociedad peruana*, Lima.

Bortoli, Giorgio. 2021. *Tower of Light. Venice-New York*. Venice: Venice Graphic Design.

Bourseul, Charles. 1854. *Transmission électrique de la parole*, L'Illustration, 26.08.1854, Paris.

Cacciari, Massimo. 1999. "Letter." Prot. no. 1931/CM/po.

Campanella, A. P. 1971. *Giuseppe Garibaldi e la tradizione garibaldina: una bibliografia dal 1807 al 1970*. Vol. 2. Ginevra, Comitato dell'Istituto Internazionale di Studi Garibaldini, 1971.

Campanella, Angelo J. 2017. *Antonio Meucci, the speaking telegraph, and the first telephone*, in https://acousticstoday.org/wp-content/uploads/2017/07/Article_3of3_from_ATCODK_3_2.pdf.

Caniggia Mauro and Luca Poggianti. 1996. *Il valdostano che inventò il telefono: Innocenzio Manzetti 1826-1877*. Aosta: Centro Studi De Tiller.

Cantini, Lorenzo, ed. 1800-1808. *Legislazione Toscana*. Vol. 19: Florence: Stamp. Albizziniana.

Caro, Robert. 1974. *The Power Broker: Robert Moses and the Fall of New York*. dew York: Knopf.

Catania, Basilio. 1990. "Alla ricerca della verità su Antonio Meucci e sulla invenzione del telefono" (Presentation, expanded, of the state of research on Antonio Meucci, on the occasion of the meeting of the Quadrato della Radio col Sig. Ministro delle Poste e Telecomunicazioni, On. Oscar Mammì, Roma, 9 July 1990), in *L'elettronica* 77.10 (October): 49–55.

Catania, Basilio. 1992. "Sulle tracce di Antonio Meucci - Appunti di viaggio." *L'Elettrotecnica* 79.10 (October): 973 – 984.

Catania, Basilio. 1994. *Antonio Meucci - L'Inventore e il suo Tempo - Da Firenze a L'Avana* (Vol. 1), Seat–Divisione STET. Rome: Editoria per la Comunicazione.

Catania, Basilio. 1996. *Antonio Meucci - L'Inventore e il suo Tempo - New York 1850-1871* (Vol. 2), Seat–Divisione STET, Turin: Editoria per la Comunicazione.

Catania, Basilio. 1999."Exhibion of telephone discovery (Havana, 1849-1999)." Celebration of the 150th Anniversary of Meucci's "talking telegraph." Havana (Cuba), November 19-25. http://www.chez basilio.org/havana 5.htm.

Catania, Basilio. 2002. "The U.S. Government Versus Alexander Graham Bell: An Important Acknowledgment for Antonio Meucci." *Bulletin of Science, Technology & Society* 22.6 (December): 426-442.

Catania, Basilio. 2003. "Antonio Meucci: How electrotherapy gave birth to telephony." European Transactions on Telecommunications 14.6 (No-vember/December): 539-552. Errata Corrigge of Fig. 12 in ETT 15.3 (May /June 2004): 293. 24 B.

Catania, Basilio. 2004."Antonio Meucci, Inventor of the Telephone: Unearth-ing the Legal and Scientific Proofs." *Bulletin of Science, Technology & Society* 24.2 (April): 115-137. Published version of a talk given at New York University, Casa Italiana Zerilli Marimò, New York, NY, October 10, 2000.

Center for Historical Studies Verrazzano, via San Martino in Valle, Greti. Greve in Chianti, Florence, online, *The letter-report of July 1524 in which the Florentine Giovanni da Verrazzano informs Francis I, King of France, of the successes.*

Ceva, Lucio. 2004. "Garibaldi militare." *Studi garibaldini* 4.3 (March): 51–60.

Chatelain, Phillipe Martin. 2013. "5 Things in NYC We Can Blame on Robert Moses." In *Untapped cities. Rediscover Your City*, December 18.

Chatelain, Phillipe Martin. 2013. "5 Things in NYC We Can Blame on Robert Moses." *Untapped cities. Rediscover Your City*, December 18. https:// untappedcities.com/2013/12/18/5-things-in-nyc-we-can-blame-on-robert-moses/.

Coppola, Ignazio. 2017. "Did you know that Garibaldi was a 'scafista'? He transported Chinese who were then sold as slaves!" *I nuovi Vespri* (15 February). https://www.inuovivespri.it/2017/02/15/sapevate-che-garibaldi-era-uno-scafista-trasportava-cinesi-che-poi-venivano-venduti-come-schiavi/.

Cowie, Ph. K. 2004. "The second exile of Giuseppe Garibaldi." *Studi garibaldini* 4.3: 61–78.

Cuneo, Giovanni Battista 1850. *Biografia di Giuseppe Garibaldi*. Turin, Tipografia Fory and Dalmazzo.

Current Population Census Bureau Estimates, United States Census Bureau, July 1, 2019. NYC planning.

Current Population Census Bureau Estimates, United States Census Bureau, July 1, 2019, NYC Planning.

Da Ponte, Lorenzo. 1976. *Memorie*. Milan: Garzanti.

de la Pezuela, Don Jacobo. 1863. "Habana, Teatro de Tacon" in *Diccionario geografico, estaditico, historico de la Isla de Cuba*. Vol. 3. 177.

de la Pezuela, Don Jacobo. 1866. *Historia de la Isla de Cuba*. Madrid: Carlos Bailly-Bailliere.

De Negri Luna, Felix. *1981. Historia Marítima de Perú*, Tomo VI. Vol 1, *La República - 1826 a 1851*, Lima: Instituto de Estudios Históricos Marítimos del Perú.

De Santis, Marco I. 2011. *Un amico di Garibaldi: Eliodoro Spech, cantante, patriota e soldato*. Molfetta: Editore Inprinting.

Dumas, Alexandre. 1860. *Memorie di Giuseppe Garibaldi*. Milan: Tipografia di Alessandro Lombardi.

Durante, Francis. 2014. *Italoamericana: The Literature of the Great Migration, 1880–1943*. Eds. Robert Viscusi, Anthony Julian Tamburri, James J. Periconi. New York: Fordham University Press.

Dwight, Theodore. 1824. *A Journal of a Tour in Italy in the Year 1821 with a Description of Gibraltar*. New York: A. Paul.

Dwight, Theodore. 1851. *The Roman Republic of 1849*. New York: R Van Dien.

Echols, Michael and Doug Arbittier. 2020. "Valentino Mott." December 20. http://medicalantiques.com/civilwar/Medical_Authors_Faculty/Mott_Vanentine.htm.

Folin, Marino. 2021. In Giorgio Bortoli, *Tower of Light*. *Venice-New York*. Venice: Venice Graphic Design.

Fortini, Pino. 1950. *Giuseppe Garibaldi: marinaio mercantile*. Rome: C. Corvo.

Frederick, H. A. 1931. "Development of the microphone," *Journal of the Acoustic Society of America* 3.1: 1-30.

Fucarino, Carmelo. 1998. "Contro la tesi di 'Garibaldi negriero'." *Rassegna storica del Risorgimento* 85: 389–397.

Galeota Capece, Francesco. 2008. Il "secondo esilio" di Giuseppe Garibaldi, in *Mediterranea Ricerche Storiche* 5.14 (December): 651–666.

Galvani, Aloysii. 1791. *De viribus electricitatis in motu musculari Commentarius*, Bononiae: Ex Typographia Instituti Scientiarum.

Garibaldi, Giuseppe. 1888. *Memorie autobiografiche*. Florence, G. Barbèra.

Garibaldi, Giuseppe. 1907. *Memoirs*, diplomatic edition from the definitive autograph edited by Ernesto Nathan. Turin, Società Tipografico-Editrice Nazionale (formerly Roux and Viarengo), XV, 444.

Garibaldi, Giuseppe. 1911.*Autobiographical Poem* (from the autograph) "Carme alla morte e altri canti inediti," published by G. E. Curatolo. Bologna: Nicola Zanichelli.

Garibaldi, Giuseppe. 1981. *Giuseppe Garibaldi, Epistolario*. Vol. III (1850–1858), Rome, Istituto per la storia del Risorgimento italiano.

Garibaldi, Giuseppe. 2002. *Memoirs*, Alberto Burgos, ed., Udine, Gaspari.

Gay, H. Nelson. 1910. "Garibaldini in Jamaica." *New Anthology* 231: 636–859.

Ghisalberti, A.M. 1980-81. "Garibaldi in Jamaica." *Nuova Antologia*. Vol. XLII.

Gnola, Davide. 2010. *Diario di bordo del capitano Giuseppe Garibaldi*. Mursia: Milan.

Gold, Kenneth M. et al. 2011. *Discovering Staten Island: A 350th Anniversary Commemorative History*. Charleston, SC: History Press.

Grosvenor, Edwin and Morgan Wesson. 2011. *Alexander Graham Bell, The Life and Times of the Man Who Invented the Telephone*. New York: Harry N. Abrams.

Harlow Alvin F. 1936. *Old Wires and New Waves: The History of the Telegraph, Telephone and Wireless*. New York: Appleton-Century. 344–348.

Huurdeman, Anton A. 2003. *The Worldwide History of Telecommunications*. New York: Wiley. 154–156.

Jacobs, Jane. 1961. *Death and the Life of America's Great Cities*. New York: Vintage Books.

Jacobs, Jane. 1961. *Death and the Life of America's Great Cities*. New York: Random House. 1961.

La Bolina, Jack (Vittorio Vecchi). 1882. *La vita e le gesta di Giuseppe Garibaldi*. Bologna: Nicola Zanichelli. 94–97.

Landini, Giancarlo. 2017. "Lorenzo Salvi." *Dizionario Biografico degli Italiani*. Rome: Treccani. s.v.

Lawrence Brodsky, Vera. 1995. *Strong on Music, The New York Music Scene in the Days of George Templeton Strong*. Vol. II Reverberations 1850-1856. Chicago: The University of Chicago Press.

Loi, Salvatore. 1982. "Garibaldi per la libertà e l'indipendenza di Cuba." *Hiram*. No. 2–3.

Maretzek, Max. 1855. *Crotchets And Quavers: Revelations of An Opera Manager in America*, New York: S. French.

Maretzek, Max. 1890. *Sharps and Flats, a sequel to Crotchets and Quavers*. Vol. I, New York, American Musician Publishing Co.

Maretzek, Max. 2006. *Further Revelations of an Opera Manager in 19th Century America: The Third Book of Memoirs*. Urbana, IL: Harmonie Park P.

Mario, White Jessie. 1884. *Garibaldi e i suoi tempi*, illustrated by Edoardo Matania. Milan, Fratelli Treves; Anastatic edition, Bononia UP, 2007.

Meucci, Antonio. 1886. *Deposition of Antonio Meucci, rendered Dec. 7, 1885-Jan. 13, 1886*, National Archives and Records Administration, Northeast Region, New York, NY. Records of the U.S. Circuit Court for the Southern District of New York. The American Bell Telephone Co. et al. vs. The Globe Telephone Co. et al. Also "Deposition of Antonio Meucci." New York Public Library (Annex), Answers, 14–17 and Meucci deposition of 11 September, answers 626–630.

"Meucci Antonio." 2010. *Dizionario Biografico degli Italiani*. Vol. 74. Rome: Istituto della Enciclopedia Italiana.

Oliva, Gaetano. 2001. "Il teatro dietro le quinte: la scenotecnica." *Scuola materna per l'educazione dell'infanzia* 88.14 (April): 18-19.

Palumbo, Agnese. 2015. *101 Women Who Made Naples Great*. Rome: Newton Compton.

Panighi, Alessio. 1903. *Documenti della Società dei Reduci dalle Patrie Battaglie e dell'Esercito*, Massa Lombarda.

Pardo Pimentel, Nicolas. 1851. *La opera italiana, ó manual del filarmónico*. Madrid: Aguado.

Quétànd, Emile. 1865. "Curiosités de la Science." *Le petit Journal* 1026 (November 22): 3.

Ramirez, Serafin. 1891. *La Habana artistica, Apuntes historicos*. Havana: E.M. de la Capitanía General.

Respighi, Luigi. 2008. *Per la priorità di Antonio Meucci nell'invenzione del telefono*. Anastatic edition Rome 1930-VIII, edited by the Comitato Nazionale per il bicentenario della nascita di Antonio Meucci. Florence: Firenze University Press.

Rosebank, Hughes C.J. 2017. *Staten Island: A Little Italy, Trying Not to Shrink, New York Times*, April 30.

Rotondi, Giuliana. 2012. *Carlo Lucarelli narrates MEU il signor telefono*, Internet Archive, Focus, Biographies, October 2012, sheet 3. Carlo Lucarelli dedicated to Meucci an episode of DEE Giallo on February 21, 2011.

Ruberto, Laura and Joseph Sciorra. 2017a. *New Italian Migrations to the United States*. Vol. 1: Politics and History since 1945. Champaign, IL: U Illinois P.

Ruberto, Laura and Joseph Sciorra. 2017b. *New Italian Migrations to the United States*. Vol. 2: Art and Culture since 1945. Champaign: U Illinois P.

Santa Cruz y Montalvo, Maria de las Mercedes. 1844. *Viaje á la Habana*. Madrid: Imprenta de la Sociedad Literaria e Tipografica.

Schiavo, Giovanni Ermenegildo. 1958. *Antonio Meucci: inventor of the Telephone*. New York: The Vigo Press.

Sciorra, Joseph. 2015. *Built with Faith: Italian American Imagination and Catholic Material Culture in New York City*.

Sciorra, Joseph. 2018. "The Our Lady of Mount Carmel Grotto in Rosebank, Staten Island." Garland Magazine, September 12. https://garland mag.com/article/the-our-lady-of-mount-carmel-grotto/.

Scirocco, Alfonso. 2001. *Garibaldi: battaglie, amori, ideali di un cittadino del mondo*. Bari: Laterza.

Sistema Museale di Caprera, Musei Garibaldini di Caprera, *Compendio Garibaldino e il Memoriale Giuseppe Garibaldi*, Isola di Caprera, Str. Cala Garibaldi. https://www.garibaldicaprera.beniculturali.it.

Staten Island 350th Anniversary Committee, Kenneth M. Gold, et al. 2011. *Discovering Staten Island: A 350th Anniversary Commemorative History*. Charleston, SC: The History Press.

Stukeley, William. 1752. *Memoirs of Sir Isaac Newton's Life*. London: N.P.

Thompson, Silvanus Phillips. 1883. *Philipp Reis: Inventor of the Telephone, A Biographical Sketch*. London, E. & F. N. Spon.

Tola, Anna. 2007. *La felicità nella libertà, Garibaldi per la libertà di Cuba*. Isola di La Maddalena: Sorba Editore.

UNIBO Magazine, Alma Mater Studiorum University of Bologna, *At the Marconi Foundation the Meucci-Catania Archive*, November 7, 2012.

Voltaire. 2011. "Quinzième lettre, Sur le système de l'attraction." *Lettres philosophiques*. Atramenta. https://www.atramenta.net/lire/oeuvre 820-chapitre-15.html.

Who is credited with inventing the telephone? in *Everyday Mysteries, Fun Science Facts*. Library of Congress.

INDEX

Academy of Fine Arts 24
Academy of the Risoluti 28
Alboni, Marietta 120
Aldini, Giovanni 55
Alighieri, Dante 104, 156
Amman, Othmar 12
Andueza, José Maria 46
Arbittier, Doug 118
Arib, Salvatore 168
Astor Opera House 120
Augier, G. Paolo 149
Avezzana, Giuseppe 73, 118, 134, 146

Babcock, Stephen M. 160
Baccani, Gaetano 30
Baguer, Nestor 53
Bandelari, Enrico 75
Barrault, Emile 130
Barsotti, Carlo 9, 156
Barzini, Luigi 96
Belau, Paul 59
Bell, Alexander Graham 23, 58, 76-78, 82, 85-107
Bellini, Vincenzo 48-49, 79
Bendelari, Enrico 80-81, 158
Bertolino, Angelo 85-86
Berti, Anselmo 79
Biagi, Alamanno 31
Bianchi, Umberto 97, 100
Bonaparte, Giuseppe 12
Bortoli, Giorgio 165, 168-170
Boston University 77, 86
Bourseul, Charles 59, 76
Brodsky, Lawrence Vera 125

Cacciari, Massimo 170
Cambiagi, Gioachino 28
Campanella, Angelo J. 109
Campanella, A. P. 79
Campeggi, Paolo Bovi 71, 117
Caniggia, Mauro 81
Cantini, Lorenzo 25
Capece, Galeota 113, 139, 143, 147
Cardano, Georlamo 72
Caro, Robert 11-12, 25
Carpanetto, Francesco 112, 136-137, 139-140
Carpeneti, Giovan Battista 138
Carrano, Francesco 73
Carroll, William 87
Casa de Recogidas 41
Casa dei Monellini 28
Casa Italiana Columbia 62
Casa Italiana Zerilli Marimò 102
Castro, Fidel 60
Castle Garden 63-64, 120
Catania, Basilo 24, 29, 34, 53, 63, 101-104, 154
Cavour, Camillo Benso 147
Center for Theatre Research "Theatre-Education" of the City of Fagnano Olona 32
Centro Gallego 59
Cerulli, Cuomo 98, 155
Ceva, Lucio 110
Chatelain, Phillipe Martin 12
Chicago-Science Hall 99
Chinese Scholar's Garden 18

Ciaccio, Carl 166
Citarotto, John 92
City University College 17
Collura, Paul J. 100
Columbia University 10, 62, 83, 115
Columbus, Christopher 2, 10, 130, 156, 163, 168
Coppola, Ignazio 143
Corbellino, Ignazio 81
Corelli, Luigi 111
Corradi, Nestore 162, 79, 82
Covarrubias, Francisco 45
Cowie, Phillip 113-114, 137-145
Crespi, Pio 96
Cross, Charles R. 92-93
Cruz y Montalvo, Santa 46
Cuneo, Giovanni Battista 118

D'Annunzio, Gabriele 163
Da Ponte, Ann 62
Da Ponte, Lorenzo 62, 79, 115
da Silva, Anna Maria Ribeiro 109-110
Da Verrazzano, Giovani 1-5, 8, 10-14, 17-18, 156, 163
Davis, Jo Anne 104
de Albornoz, Mariano Carrillo 42
de Andueza, José María 46
de la Concha, José Gutiérrez 39
de Medici, Carlo 29
de Medici, Cosimo III 25, 29-30
de Medici, Ferdinando II 28
de Negri, Pedro 138, 146-147
De Niro, Robert 13
de la Pezuela, Jacobo 36-37, 40, 42, 45, 47, 49
de la Rive, Auguste 55

de Santillana, Giorgio Diaz 100
De Santis, Marco I. 70
Dessaa, Mary 79
Donizetti, Gaetano 49, 79
d'Orléans, Luisa 29
Dumas, Alexandre 73, 130
Dwight, Theodore 73

Echols, Michael 118
Ellis Island 22, 68, 120
Engel, Eliot 104

Ferdinand VII 35, 43
Fermi, Enrico 100
Fernando VII 54
Ferrini, Ettore 163
Feyerabend, Ernst 100
Ficini, Luigi 26
Folin, Marino 168
Foresti, Felice 115, 118-119, 134, 146, 148
Fossella, Vito 105-106
Franci, Filippo 28
Francis I 1, 8, 10
Frederich, H.A. 97
Frederick William III 97, 120
Free Academy of Painting and Drawing 43
French Academy of Sciences 55
Froscianti, Giovanni 151
Fry, Edward 69, 120, 122

Galeota, Capece 113, 139, 143, 147
Galvani, Luigi 54-56
Gargani, Luigi 28
Garibaldi, Giuseppe 61, 67, 69-74, 79-81, 95, 98, 106, 108-153, 155-169

Garibaldi Memorial 22, 98, 161
Garibaldi-Meucci Museum 95,
   100, 106, 125, 151, 155, 157, 161
Gazque, Ramón 48
Gear, Emily 106
George Washington Bridge 13
Ghisalberti, A.M. 137
Gnola, Davide 126-127
Golden Gate Bridge 16
Gran Teatro de La Habana 60
Grandi, Angelo Zilio 85
Gray, Elisha 78, 86, 89
Grosvenor, Edwin 88
Guazzoni, Enrico 23, 107
Guerrazzi, Francesco
   Domenico 27
Guevara, Che 60

Hagg, Dwight 148
Harlow Alvin F. 80
Haussmann, Georges Eugène 12
Herzen, Aleksandr 149
Historical Archives of the
   Accademia Nazionale dei
   Lincei 99
Hitler, Adolf 99
Hospice of San Filippo Neri 28
Hospice of the Quarconi 28
House Museum of Alice
   Austen 18, 28
Hubbard, Gardiner 85, 89
Hudson, Henry 1
Hugo, Victor 130
Huurdeman, Anton 80

Idvorsky, Pupin Michele 83
Institution of Engineering and
   Technology 99

Isabella II 35
Italian American Historical
   Society 11, 155-156
Izaguirre, Joaquin Muños 42

Jacobs, Jane 12
Jameson, Annie 98
John D. Calandra Italian
   American Institute 21

Kelly, James Angelo 11
Kennedy, John F. 12, 84
Kennedy, Robert 12
Koch, Edward I. 156

La Bolina, Jack 142-143, 147, 150
LaCorte, John N. 11-12
La Cour, Poul 78
La Guarida, Fiorello 155
Lanari, Alessandro 28, 31
Landini, Giancarlo 69
La Pergola 28, 40, 50-51, 122
La Scala 47-48, 69
League of Nations 98
Libera, Adalberto 99
Liceo Artistico y Literation 48
Lincoln, Abraham 151, 157
Llagostera, Bernardo 41
Loi, Salvatore 138
Lucarelli, Carlo 23, 27

Magellan, Ferdinand 2
Manzetti, Innocenzo 81
Marconi, Guglielmo 84, 98-100,
   104, 107, 154
Maretzek, Max 37-39, 63-67,
   119-125
Margheri, Dante 28-29

Maria Carolina of Saxony 25
Mario, E.A. 114
Mario, Jessie White 118, 124, 135, 138, 147-149
Maroncelli, Piero 62
Martí, Pancho 37, 40, 52, 63, 65, 69
Marty y Torrens, Francisco 36-40, 44, 47, 49-53, 63, 65-67, 123
Massaro, Dominic R. 102
Mauro, Caniggia 81
Mayo, Antonio 45
Mazzani, Giuseppe 27, 109, 118, 130, 147, 149-150
Melena, Elpis 73
Menotti, Ciro 27, 110
Merloni, Roberto 159
Meucci, Amadigi 23, 25-26
Meucci, Antonio 23-34, 51-58, 61-70, 72-75, 78-107, 118-138, 146, 151, 153-159, 161-163, 166, 169
Mill, John Stuart 130
Mochi, Maria Matilde Ester 34, 51
Moncada, Francesco 100, 155
Moore, Clement 62
Moriño, Antonio 38
Moses, Robert 11-12
Mott, Valentino 117
Musei Garibaldini di Caprera 125
Museo Centrale del Risorgimento 137, 158
Museum of Science and Industry 99

Museum of the History of Science 99
Mussolini, Benito 28, 96, 98, 163

Napoleon, Louis 42, 111
National Library of Florence 29
National Museum of Science 100
Naum, Abraham 168
Newton, Isaac 55, 57
New York University 102, 117, 156

O'Donnell, Leopoldo 42, 56
Oliva, Gaetano 32
Opéra National de Paris 47
Oudinot, Nicolas 111
Our Lady of Mount Carmel Grotto 21

Palacin y Abarca, Mariano Ricafort 35
Palumbo, Agnese 118
Park Theatre 62
Pastacaldi, Michele 115, 119, 134, 147
Pastor, Manuel 54
Patanelli, Raffaele 79
Patrik. H.H. 89
Patrizi, Ettore 97
Pavese, Luigi 23, 107
Pellico, Silvio 115
Pepi, Maria Domenico 24
Pimentel, Nicolas Pardo 45
Pintó, Ramón 48
Poggianti, Luca 81
Popov, Aleksandr Stepanovič 98

Prieto, Andrés 43
Provenzal, Giulio 99
Pupin, Michele 83, 101

Raimondi, Maria Rosa Nicoletta 145
Ramirez, Serafin 40-43, 45-46, 48-49
Reis, Johann Philipp 59, 76, 77, 80
Respighi, Luigi 56, 71, 73, 91, 94, 100
Reymond, Emil Du Bois 55
Robert F. Kennedy Bridge (Triborough Bridge) 11-12
Rockefeller, Nelson 12
Rosebank, Hughes C.J. 22
Rossi, Adolfo 135
Rossi, Carlo 120
Rossini, Gioachino 48-49, 62, 79
Rotondi, Giuliana 23, 27

Salvi, Lorenzo 40, 66-69, 119-123, 125
Sanders, Thomas 85
Santa Cruz y Montalvo, Maria de las Mercedes 46
Schiaffino, Simone 146
Schiavo, Giovanni Ermenegildo 93, 101
Schneider, Amalia 62
Sciame, Joseph 19, 166
Sciorra, Joseph 21
Scirocco, Alfonso 109
Silvestri, Bartolomeo 30
Society of Our Lady of Mount Carmel 21
Sontag, Mme. Herriette 120-122

Sorel, Albert 55
Spech, Eliodoro 69-70
St. George Theatre 17
St. John's University 17-19, 21
St. Joseph's School 21
St. Mary's School 21
Stukeley, William 57
Susini, Antonio 111

Tacca, Ferdinando 29
Tacón y Rosique, Miguel 35
Tagliabue, Giuseppe 160
Teatro Carcano 49
Teatro de Villanueva 44
Teatro della Quarconia 28
Teatro della Pergola 28-29
Teatro Giglio 28
Teatro Principal 36, 50
Teatro San Carlo 49
Teatro Stabile 50
Theater Alfieri 28
Theater Goldoni 28
the Liceo 40, 48-49
the Lyceum 42
the National Cinema 28
Thompson, Silvanus Phillips 77
Timpanaro, Sebastiano 100
Tola, Anna 137
Travolta, John 13
Tremeschin, Angelo Antonio 85
Trentini, Girolamo 25
Tresca, Carlo 96
Trombetta, Domenico 97
Turini, Giovanni 152, 156-157, 164

Ulman. A.P. 97
Università Cattolica del Sacro Cuore 32

University of Bologna 54, 55,
    69, 71, 117, 126
University of Wisconsin 160

Valerio, Giuseppe 148
Vallone, Peter 102-103
Varley, Cromwell 78
Vecchi, Augusto Vittorio 142, 144
Verdi, Giuseppe 35, 79, 156
Vermay, Francisco Dionisio
    Vives 43
Vermay, Juan Bautista 42
Verrazzano Narrows Bridge
    10-18, 163
Vespucci, Amerigo 2, 10
Vittorio Emanuele III 99, 142, 155
Viviani, Luigi Maria 31
Voltaire 57
von Helmholtz, Hermann 88
von Reichdenback, Karl 73

Wagner College 17
Wallace, William James 92-93
Washington, George 14-15, 157

Yale University 84

Ximenes, Ettore 156

ABOUT THE AUTHOR

Carmelo Fucarino

Carmelo Fucarino graduated in classical literature from the University of Palermo and taught Latin and Greek language and literature at the "G. Garibaldi" classical high school in the same city. Sensitive to poetry, he published poetry and essays in journals dedicated to Italian literature and carried out a wide and continuous activity as an essayist in the field of classical studies. Today he has expanded his field of inquiry to local history to ethnology and Sicilian folk traditions.

The author of more than one dozen books, some titles are: *Se nulla cambiò: i garibaldini a Prizzi* (Franco Cesati Editore, 2015); *Il Genio Palermo vita e morte e miracoli di un dio* (Thule, 2017); *Virgilio esoterico: segni di culti misterici* (Carlo Saladino, 2022); *Da Pitagora al veganismo: l'astensione dagli esseri viventi* (Aracne, 2020); *Palcoscenico. Rivisitazioni tra lirica ed opera (2009-2022)* (Thule, 2022).

ABOUT THE ARTIST

William J. Castello

Born in Flatbush, Brooklyn, William J. Castello began his art career early in life. By age nine the Brooklyn Public Library (Flatbush Branch) allowed him to display his realistic portraits for over six months. Bill went to Nazareth High School from 1972-1975. He attended St. John's University where he honed his skills and earned his Bachelor of Fine Arts.

He has had one-man exhibits at St. John's, Columbia Univ., the Gross Gallery, Queens, and took part in many more in the metropolitan area. After collage he found a job as a graphic journalist at the New York World Headquarters of the Associated Press where he published his news-related art and stories to over 8,500 periodicals, worldwide, daily. He retired after a 35-year career.

Prof. William John Castello currently teaches Communication Arts at St. John's University in New York City. He has turned much of his effort to perfecting his personal art and produced over a dozen new portraits on canvas including Fr. Vincent Capodanno, Steven Siller, and the portrait of Garibaldi and Meucci on permanent loan to the Garibaldi-Meucci Museum. He also produced thousands of pencil/graphite-on-tan paper portraits. Many of these were featured at the GMM. Prof. Castello is currently the artist-in-residence, and contributor to the GMM. He has researched, written, and curated all the current historical exhibits in our museum.

OTHER CONTRIBUTORS

SIÂN GIBBY is Communications Writer-Editor at the John D. Calandra Italian American Institute. She is co-editor with Tamburri of *Diversity in Italian Studies* (2021) and, with Joseph Sciorra and Tamburri, co-editor of *This Hope Sustains the Scholar* (2021). Her translations from Italian include Quinto Antonelli's *Intimate History of the Great War: Letters, Diaries, and Memoirs from Soldiers on the Front* (Bordighera Press, 2016) and Luigi Fontanella's novel *The God of New York* (Bordighera Press, 2021).

Comm. JOSEPH SCIAME is Vice President for Community Relations at St. John's University. As such, he interacts as a key University representative with various community groups and organizations surrounding the University campuses. Among his many roles beyond the University, he currently serves as President of the Sons of Italy Foundation (Washington, DC) and President of the Italian Heritage and Cultural Committee Inc., NY. He was awarded the rank of Commendatore Order of Merit of the Republic of Italy and Cavaliere Gran Croce of the House of Savoy.

ANTHONY JULIAN TAMBURRI is Dean of the John D. Calandra Italian American Institute (Queens College, CUNY) and Distinguished Professor of European Languages and Literatures. His most recent publication is *A Politics of [Self-]Omission: The Italian/American Challenge in A Post-George Floyd Age* (2022). In 2010, he was awarded the rank of Cavaliere Order of Merit of the Republic of Italy.

Diaspora

As **diaspora** *is the dispersion or spread of people from their original homeland, this book series takes its name in the intellectual spirit of willful dispersion of subject matter and thought. It is dedicated to publishing those studies that in various and sundry ways either speak to or offer new methods of analysis of the Italian diaspora.*

Carmelo Fucarino. *Two Italian Geniuses in New York: Broken American Dreams*. ISBN 978-1-955995-05-4. 2023

Anthony Julian Tamburri, ed. *Re-Thinking* The Godfather *50 Years Later*. ISBN 978-1-955995-06-1. 2024

Anthony Socci. *United We Stand. Pre WW II-Chronicles of the Italian Colony of Stamford*. ISBN 978-1-955995-07-8. 2024

Antonio D'Alfonso. *I Could Have Been a Contender. (On Five Films)*. ISBN 978-1-955995-09-2. 2024

Antonio Vitti and Anthony Julian Tamburri, eds. *Studi mediterranei: bellezze e misteri. Mediterranean Studies: Beauty and Mystery*. ISBN 978-1-955995-10-8. 2024

Luigi Fontanella. *Bertgang. Fanatasia onirica*. Translation by Michael Palma. ISBN 978-1-955995-11-05. 2025. Poetry

Mark Saba. *The Shoemaker*. ISBN 978-1-955995-12-2. 2025. Fiction

Anthony Julian Tamburri, ed. *Living Biculturalism, Writing Transculturalism: Essays in Honor of Luigi Fontanella*. ISBN 978-1-955995-13-9. 2025

Antonio Vitti and Anthony Julian Tamburri, eds. *Studi mediterranei: bellezze e misteri. Cultura mediterranea: variazioni su un tema*. ISBN 978-1-955995-15-3. 2025.

www.ingramcontent.com/pod-product-compliance
Lightning Source LLC
Chambersburg PA
CBHW071422160426
43195CB00013B/1773